The Natives Chal_ _ _ _ _ _

Edited and compiled
by Iain Martin &
Vicky Brown

natives.co.uk
knowledge is powder

First published 2005

Written and Compiled by Iain Martin & Vicky Brown
Design by Qanuk Publishing & Design Ltd
Printed in Singapore

Published by Natives.co.uk Ltd
17 Linstead House
9 Disraeli Rd
London SW15 2DR

Tel - 08700 463377

ISBN 0-9545625-1-8

Special thanks to Marie-France Goddard, Susie Burt and Tony Cave

contents

photo credits

Why a chalet cook book?

This is no ordinary recipe book that you might expect to find from the Jamies or Delias of this world (!). The Natives Chalet Cook Book does what it says on the tin - recipes for successfully running a chalet for a winter season.

Not only does it contain recipes for any chalet, and for every taste, it's also packed with helpful tips, conversions, translations, and all the things that will help you complete a successful season.

Natives are all experienced season workers, so the dinner party recipes you'll find in this book are all tried and tested, will work at altitude, and are simple to follow.

Indeed, these recipes work just as well in the home as in a chalet, and for that reason, this book should have a place on any kitchen shelf, whether you are a complete beginner or a budding gourmet cook!

Useful Tips:

'GF' indicates gluten free

indicates preparation time

indicates cooking time

A brief history of Natives:
Natives started as a project by founder Iain Martin, who was fed up with season workers being misrepresented in so-called 'documentaries' on TV. The website launched in the heat of the dot.com boom in April 1999. Traffic soon grew and has continued to grow as season workers, job seekers and snowsports lovers alike have come to the site.

Now Natives serves over 600,000 page impressions a month to more than 120,000 unique users, making it the UK's leading snowsports community. More season workers get their jobs through Natives than any other source. Our sister site - ResortJobs.co.uk - is beginning to take the same role for summer work.

working as a chalet host

When chalet holidays first became popular in the 1980's, young women (often referred to as 'Sloanes') flocked to the Alps to work in a new role - as a 'chalet girl'. Cooking and cleaning for guests in chalets rented for a season, these chalet girls provided a 'home from home' environment that could not be found in hotels.

The chalet holiday concept has grown enormously over the last twenty years, and now, every winter, thousands of staff are employed by tour operators and independent companies to run chalets. And with the advent of equal opportunities these jobs have long since been open not only to non-Sloanes, but even to men!

What does a chalet host do?

Usually working from early-December to mid-April, chalet hosts provide breakfast, afternoon tea and a three or four course evening meal, 6 days per week, for up to 12 guests. In addition, they are expected to keep the chalet spotlessly clean, budget and shop for or order the food, and keep basic accounts.

Chalets vary in size from 6 - 50 bed properties. Generally where chalets are greater than 10-bed, assistants are also employed.

Sounds like a lot of hard work!

Running a chalet is hard work and requires bags of stamina, patience and a good sense of humour! It does have its advantages, however. Once a routine is established, staff can be finished and on the mountain by 11am, through to 4pm most days, making it one of the best positions in the Alps in terms of skiing/boarding time.

What package would a chalet host expect?

Employers generally provide a weekly/monthly wage, food, accommodation, lift pass, ski equipment, insurance, and return travel to resort from the UK. Good chalet staff can also expect regular tips from guests.

How do I find a job as a chalet host?

Between June and November, you can apply for hundreds of chalet positions online at www.natives.co.uk.

You will need good cooking experience or a qualification, and the confidence to take on the role.

If you don't have a cooking background, then attending a cookery course will significantly increase your chances of finding a chalet job. Natives run regular chalet cookery courses from May through to October - see page 82 for further details - and guarantee jobs to successful students.

canapés, soups and starters

Sometimes it's the little things that make all the difference. The main course is probably the most important part of any meal, but you never get a second chance to make a first impression - so your canapés, soups and starters are just as important.

Canapés
Many chalet companies offer canapés, generally served with pre-dinner drinks at around 7.30pm in the chalet. Often chalet hosts panic unnecessarily about canapés and struggle with ideas, so we have included a range of ideas to last the chalet week, all of which can be prepared quickly and easily.

Soups and starters
Starters should be varied throughout the week. For example, you should avoid serving soup or salad more than twice in any one week.

For variety, you should also try to avoid re-using the same ingredients during a meal, for example, goats cheese salad starter, a main course stuffed with brie, followed by cheesecake for dessert.

Soups are a good starter to serve on a changeover day, as they will bubble away while you're busy with cleaning, and won't be ruined if the coach is late! Dress up simple soups with homemade croutons, a swirl of cream, or a sprinkling of parsley.

SMOKED SALMON TRIANGLES

🥄 15 minutes
⬛ n/a

1 loaf sliced wholemeal or brown bread
Approx. 3oz/75g butter

6 slices smoked salmon
A few black olives

Spread butter thinly on 10 slices of bread. Trim off the crust and cut each slice into 4 small triangles.

Cut each salmon slice into 2, to fit the size of the bread slices and place on the buttered bread.

Place an olive segment on each one.

Arrange the triangles slightly overlapping each other on the serving dish.

FILO BASKETS
Serves 10-12

🥄 10 minutes
⬛ 15 minutes

1 packet of filo pastry
Greaseproof paper

Sunflower oil

First, cut your greaseproof paper into 10-12 small squares about 3cm/2 inches square.

To make the filo baskets, cut the filo pastry into 10cm/4 inch squares.

Take one of the squares of greaseproof paper and lay flat, brush with a little oil.

Next place a square of pastry on top of the greaseproof paper and brush with a little oil. Take another square and place on top of the previous one but at an angle and brush with oil. Take a third square and place on top at an angle to the second, brush with a little oil. You should now have a shape roughly resembling a star.

> You can fill your baskets with just about anything savoury and sweet.
> Some suggestions:
> - Avocado, mayonnaise and crispy bacon
> - Prawn, mayonnaise and melon
> - Chicken, cucumber and mango
> - Red onion, feta cheese and tomato

Next mould your star of filo pastry over the top of an upturned tea/coffee cup, jam jar or anything which has a base about 7cm/3 inches wide with the greaseproof paper on the underside.

Place each cup/jar onto a baking tray and put into a pre-heated oven at 200°C for 10-15 mins until the filo pastry has turned crisp and a light golden brown.

Remove from the oven and carefully take each basket off the top of the cup/jar, remove the square of greaseproof paper from the inside and place onto a cooling rack.

Store in an airtight container and use within a few days.

Note: The filo pastry dries out extremely quickly when exposed to the air, so while you are assembling each basket it is best to lay a clean, damp j-cloth over the top of the squares to keep them from drying out and turning brittle.

HONEY-GLAZED COCKTAIL SAUSAGES (GF)

🍽 **5 minutes**
🔲 **25 minutes**

20 fresh cocktail sausages
20 cocktail sticks (optional)

5 tbsp clear honey

In a bowl, toss the sausages in the honey until they are completely coated.

Cover and leave to marinate in the fridge for 30 minutes or more.

Place them on a greased baking tray and bake at 180°C for 20-25 minutes, turning them over occasionally to get them evenly browned.

Serve hot, preferably with a cocktail stick pricked in each one.

MINI VOL-AU-VENTS WITH CHEESE AND CHIVES

🍽 **5 minutes**
🔲 **8 minutes**

1 packet frozen mini vol-au-vent cases
1 bunch of fresh chives, finely chopped

1 large box soft cheese spread
1 small jar of capers

Bake the vol-au-vent cases according to instructions on the packet (usually about 200°C for about 8 minutes). Leave to cool.

As near as possible to serving time, beat all the cheese portions together until creamy and smooth.

Incorporate the chopped chives, reserving some for sprinkling.

Stuff the cases with the mixture, place a caper or two on top of each one and sprinkle the remaining chives on top.

MARINATED OLIVES (GF)

🍽 **15 minutes**
🔲 **n/a**

700ml extra virgin olive oil
8oz/200g black olives
8oz/200g stuffed olives
Finely pared zest of 1 orange, shredded

8oz/200g green olives
2 tbsp coriander seeds
A few fresh coriander sprigs

If the olives have not been stoned, use a rolling pin to strike each black and green olive gently, to split but not crush it. Arrange the olives in layers in a 1.2 litre glass jar. Sprinkle each layer with coriander seeds and orange zest. Tuck a few sprigs of coriander down the side of the jar.

Warm the olive oil in a saucepan to release the aroma, then pour enough into the jar to cover the olives completely.

Tapping the jar to release any air bubbles, seal tightly and allow to cool. Leave in a cool dark place for about 1 month to mature.

SMOKED SALMON PÂTÉ (GF)
Serves 4

🥄 15 minutes
▭ n/a

8oz/200g smoked salmon
150ml double or whipping cream
Juice of a lemon

2oz/50g melted butter
Lemon (to garnish)
Salt and pepper

Blend together the salmon, lemon juice, seasoning, butter and add the cream until a smooth paste is formed. Divide out into ramekin dishes or refrigerate until the mixture goes firm.

Using two dessert spoons take a small amount of the mixture and shape into small cigars.

Use 3 portions per person and garnish with lemon and parsley and serve with toast and butter.

PÂTÉ WITH FRENCH TOAST
Serves 10

🥄 15 minutes
▭ 20 minutes

10 slices of pâté (mushroom or similar)
A few lettuce leaves for decoration

1 loaf of sliced sandwich loaf

Slice your pâté into 10 slices and set aside.

Pre-heat your grill to 200°C and cut the crusts off about 10 slices of bread. Place onto a baking sheet and put under the grill until they turn slightly crisp and golden brown on the upper side, turn over and brown the other side.

Next, carefully cut each slice of bread in half through the middle so you halve the thickness of the bread. Then cut in half again diagonally so you make triangles.

> This is a very easy starter to do, ideal for a Saturday evening if clients are arriving late or you have a major disaster with something else!! You can buy some very good pâtés from the supermarket, but your guests will enjoy one you have made even more.

Place the triangles of toast back onto the baking tray and toast the non-cooked side - the corners will curl inwards as they brown. Remove and cool on a wire rack.

Serve your pâté on a plate with a bit of lettuce for decoration and a couple of slices of French toast per plate. Serve the remaining toast in a basket on the table. Use 3 portions per person and garnish with lemon and parsley and serve with toast and butter.

DEVILS ON HORSEBACK (GF)

🥄 5 minutes
▭ 20 minutes

20 pre-soaked (ready to use) stoned prunes
20 cocktail sticks (optional)

20 bacon rashers

Roll a bacon rasher around each prune. Place the 'devils' on a greased baking tray and bake at 180°C for 20 minutes turning them over once after 10 minutes.

Serve hot or cold, preferably with a cocktail stick pricked in each one.

CARROT AND CORIANDER SOUP
Serves 6

🍴 10 minutes
🍳 30 minutes

7oz/175g leeks
150ml natural yoghurt or soured cream
2oz/50g butter
1 tsp plain flour

Salt and pepper
18oz/450g carrots, peeled
2 tsp ground coriander
1 litre vegetable stock

To Garnish
Coriander leaves

Croûtons

Slice the leeks and carrots. Heat the butter in a large saucepan. Add the vegetables, cover the pan and cook gently for 5-10 minutes or until the vegetables begin to soften but not colour.

Stir in the coriander and flour and cook for 1 minute. Add the stock and bring to the boil, stirring. Season, reduce the heat, cover and simmer for 20 minutes or until the ingredients are quite tender.

Leave the soup to cool slightly, then purée in a blender or food processor until quite smooth. Return the soup to the pan and stir in the yoghurt. Check seasoning and reheat gently; do not boil. Serve garnished with coriander leaves and croûtons.

FRENCH ONION SOUP

🍴 10 minutes
🍳 45 minutes

½ medium French stick
3 onions, peeled
2oz/50g butter
3oz/75g Gruyère cheese, grated
900ml beef stock

1 bay leaf
Salt and pepper
1 tbsp flour

Slice the onions thinly. Melt the butter in a saucepan, add the onions and cook gently for 15-20 minutes until dark golden brown.

Stir in the flour and cook, stirring, for 1 minute. Stir in the stock, seasoning and bay leaf. Bring to the boil, cover and simmer for 30 minutes.

Cut the loaf diagonally into 1cm (½ inch) slices and toast lightly on both sides. Place 2 slices in each ovenproof soup bowl. Ladle the hot soup over the bread, discarding the bay leaf.

Sprinkle liberally with the cheese to form a thick layer over the bread. Place under a hot grill until the cheese is melted and bubbling. Serve immediately.

VEGETABLE SOUP (GF)
Serves 10

🥄 10 minutes
▭ 50 minutes

2 onions, finely chopped
2 tsp Herbes de Provence
1½ litres vegetable stock
4 tbsp chopped fresh chervil
1½ kg seasonal vegetables to include potato, peppers, carrots and 4 or 5 others

3oz/75g butter
Salt and pepper
100ml single cream

In a large cooking pot, melt the butter and fry the onions gently until soft, but not brown. Add all the other vegetables, herbs, salt and pepper and cook gently, stirring, for 2 minutes. Add the stock. Bring to the boil while stirring. Turn down the heat and simmer gently, covered, for 45 minutes.

You can either blend the soup before serving or serve the small vegetable pieces. Serve hot in individual bowls with a swirl of cream and a sprinkling of chopped fresh chervil.

Note: either cut into large pieces if you intend to blend the soup or into very small pieces or cubes if you intend to serve it without blending it.

CREAMY LEEK AND POTATO SOUP (GF)
Serves 10

🥄 10 minutes
▭ 50 minutes

2 onions, finely chopped
10 potatoes, peeled and cubed (small)
3oz/75g butter
Salt and pepper
5 leeks, thoroughly washed and sliced (small)

200ml double cream
4 tbsp chopped fresh parsley
2 tsp Herbes de Provence
1½ litres vegetable stock

In a large cooking pot, melt the butter and fry the onions gently until soft, but not brown. Add the potatoes, leeks, herbs, salt and pepper and cook gently, stirring, for 2 minutes. Add the stock. Bring to the boil while stirring. Turn down the heat and simmer gently, covered, for 45 minutes.

Just before serving, add the cream to the pot and cook for 2 or 3 minutes.

Serve immediately in individual bowls, ladling out equal amounts of vegetable pieces and liquid, with a sprinkling of chopped fresh parsley on top.

CROÛTONS

🥄 5 minutes
▭ 5-10 minutes

3 tbsp olive oil
5 slices of bread, cut into cubes

Salt and pepper

In a roasting tin, mix the oil, salt and pepper together. Turn the bread cubes over briskly in the mixture until coated, but not soaked with oil.

Bake in the oven at 180°C for 10-15 minutes, tossing the croûtons a couple of times during baking.

LEEK AND ROQUEFORT TART
Serves 10

🍳 10 minutes
🔲 45 minutes

2oz/50g butter
3 large eggs, beaten
9oz/225g Roquefort cheese
Shortcrust pastry made with 9oz/225g flour (see recipe on page 69)
OR 1 block of frozen Shortcrust pastry

1kg of leeks, thinly sliced
300ml double cream
Salt and pepper

Roll out the pastry on a lightly floured surface and use an oiled/greased 25cm (10 inch) spring-release cake tin which should be at least ¾ inch deep. Cover and chill while making the filling.

To make the filling, melt the butter in a large heavy-based pan. Add the leeks and cook, stirring over a high heat for 2-3 minutes or until they begin to soften. Cover tightly and cook very gently for 10-15 minutes until the leeks are nicely soft.

In a bowl beat together the eggs, cream and the cheese, broken into pieces; and season with salt and pepper. Place the leeks into the pastry case and pour over the egg mixture.

Place the flan tin on a baking sheet and bake in a preheated oven at 200°C for 15 minutes. Then turn down the oven to 180°C for a further 30 minutes until the pastry is golden brown and the tart is set. Serve warm or cold.

FRENCH STYLE BREADED GARLIC MUSHROOMS
Serves 10

🍳 10 minutes
🔲 15 minutes

30-40 medium/large fresh mushrooms
1 loaf sliced white bread/French stick
A little butter and olive oil

1 whole garlic clove
1 egg
Salt and pepper

Clean or peel your mushrooms and remove the stalks.

Make your breadcrumbs by placing the bread into a mixer and process until you have nice fine crumbs. Pour into a bowl. Crack the egg into another bowl and beat lightly with a fork and add your seasoning.

Next coat each mushroom with the egg and then drop into your breadcrumbs and coat evenly. Place onto a baking tray.

Once all your mushrooms are coated, peel and crush your garlic clove over the top of the mushrooms. Add a bit more salt and pepper and drizzle with a little olive oil and 3-4 cubes of butter.

Cook in a pre-heated oven at 200°C for 15 minutes or until your mushrooms are just tender and the breadcrumbs have turned golden.

Serve immediately.

Note: the breadcrumbs tend to get very stuck up with the egg so do not put all of them into the bowl at once. Keep some back so you can keep adding fresh.

TOMATO, BASIL AND MOZZARELLA
ON A GARLIC CROÛTON
Serves 10

🍷 10 minutes
🍳 35 minutes

1-2 French sticks (preferably a day old)	Olive oil
2 cloves garlic	8-10 medium sized tomatoes
4-5 packets of Italian mozzarella cheese	Fresh basil leaves, chopped

Pre-heat your oven to 180°C. Slice the French bread into 1.5-2cm slices on the diagonal, allowing for 2 slices per person, a total of 20 slices. Lay on a baking tray and drizzle the olive oil over each slice, then peel and cut the garlic cloves in half and rub each slice of bread with the garlic. Turn the slices and repeat on the other side.

> This is a very easy starter to do, the croûtons can be prepared a little ahead and then the tomato and mozzarella can be placed on top and left ready to put in the oven.

Place in the oven for 15-20 minutes turning once until the bread is just crispy and has taken on a bit of colour on both sides.

Remove and leave to cool. This can be done up to 2 hours in advance but not much more as the bread will go stale and rock hard!

Slice your tomatoes and mozzarella into thin slices and once the bread slices have cooled lay alternate slices of tomato and mozzarella on to each croûton, 2 slices of tomato and mozzarella per croûton.

Place in the oven at 180°C for 10-15 minutes until the tomato is just soft and the cheese is beginning to melt. Remove from oven and sprinkle over your chopped basil leaves and drizzle with a little olive oil.

Serve immediately on a plate decorated with a little lettuce. As an alternative, you could use sun dried tomatoes, or half a cherry tomato.

ASPARAGUS TIPS WITH
LEMON BUTTER (GF)
Serves 10

🍷 5 minutes
🍳 5 minutes

4oz/100g clarified butter	Juice and zest of 1 lemon
2-3 bunches of asparagus (4-5 spears per person)	

Melt the butter in a saucepan (or microwave) then allow to settle for a few minutes until the whey (the thicker, whiter liquid) has settled to the bottom. Pour off the clear yellow butter from the top into another bowl and discard the whey.

Finely grate the zest of your lemon and also add the juice to the butter and season.

Cook your asparagus in boiling salted water until the spears are tender, then drain.

Serve the asparagus on individual plates and pour over a little of the lemon butter. Serve the rest of the butter in a separate dish.

MOROCCAN ORANGE AND COUSCOUS SALAD

15 minutes
n/a

Serves 4-6

7oz/175g couscous
1 bunch spring onions, chopped finely
1 small green pepper, seeded and chopped
7oz/175g can of chick peas rinsed and drained
Lettuce leaves to serve

2 oranges
10cm piece cucumber
Salt and pepper
2oz/50g sultanas or raisins
Fresh mint sprigs to garnish

Dressing
Finely grated rind of 1 orange
150ml natural yoghurt

1 tbsp chopped fresh mint

Put the couscous into a bowl and cover with boiling water. Leave it to soak for about 15 minutes to swell the grains, then stir with a fork to separate them.

Add the spring onions, green pepper, cucumber, chick peas and sultanas or raisins to the couscous, stirring to combine. Season well with salt and pepper.

To make the dressing, mix together the orange rind, mint and yoghurt. Pour over the couscous mixture and stir well.

Using a sharp serrated knife, remove the peel and pith from the oranges. Cut the oranges into segments removing all the membrane.

Arrange the lettuce leaves on 4 serving plates. Divide the couscous mixture between the plates and arrange the orange segments on top.

Garnish with sprigs of fresh mint and serve.

SALADE SAVOYARDE (GF)

15 minutes
n/a

Serves 10

8 hard-boiled eggs cut into quarters
2 packets of lardons (diced bacon)
8 cherry tomatoes or 4-5 regular tomatoes

Mixed salad
1 large slice of Roquefort cheese

Hard boil your eggs and cut into quarters.

Halve your cherry tomatoes or quarter the regular tomatoes.

Fry the lardons until nice and crispy.

Chop the Roquefort cheese into small cubes.

Arrange the salad on each plate and place all the other ingredients onto the salad decoratively. You can add other things into this salad such as cucumber, grated carrot or black olives.

main courses

Main courses in chalets should always consist of either a meat or fish dish, accompanied by some form of carbohydrate and two types of vegetable (see page 39 for vegetable accompaniments).

A variety of different types of meat and fish should be used throughout the week to avoid repetition, and certain types of dish should be avoided, for example:

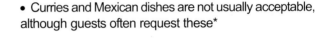

- Mince should not generally be used as part of a main dish, as it tends to be thought of as a 'budget' food

- Pasta dishes are not acceptable as main courses

- Curries and Mexican dishes are not usually acceptable, although guests often request these*

Your employer should give you specific guidelines at the beginning of the season as to what is acceptable. Typically if guests request a particular dish, then it is fine to serve it, provided the whole party agree.

This chapter is full of tasty main course recipes, including chicken, duck, lamb, pork, beef, and fish dishes.

CHICKEN BREASTS WITH SUN-DRIED TOMATOES, TARRAGON AND PAPRIKA (GF)
Serves 6

5 minutes
15 minutes

6 skinless chicken breast fillets
12-14 sun-dried tomatoes soaked in oil
2 heaped tsp paprika
1 large clove of garlic
1 tbsp fresh tarragon

2oz/50g butter
8 tbsp lemon juice
300 ml/½ pint double cream
Salt and pepper

Slice the chicken thinly and place in a bowl with the lemon juice, paprika, garlic and tarragon. Coat the chicken with the mixture and leave for 30 minutes to marinate in the fridge.

Melt the butter in a frying pan, add the chicken and fry for 8-10 minutes. Slice each sun-dried tomato into 3-4 pieces and add to the chicken. Stir in the double cream and bring to the boil, stirring for 2-3 minutes.

Season to taste with salt and freshly ground black pepper. Serve immediately. Good accompaniments to this are tagliatelle or new potatoes with green vegetables.

SATAY CHICKEN FILLETS
Serves 6

10 minutes
15 minutes

6 chicken fillets
Handful of freshly chopped coriander

Butter for frying

Marinade
1 small onion, chopped
½ tsp ginger
2 tsp chilli powder
2 tsp dark brown sugar
1 tbsp vegetable oil

1 garlic clove, crushed
2 tbsp soy sauce
1 tsp ground coriander
1 tbsp lemon or lime juice
Peanut butter (optional)

Prepare the marinade by putting all the ingredients in a blender and blending to a fine consistency. Reserve about a glassful of marinade if you wish to make a satay sauce later.

Pour the remaining marinade into a bowl. Add the chicken fillets and toss them in the marinade until they are completely coated. Cover the bowl tightly and refrigerate for at least an hour, but ideally prepare this in the morning for the evening meal.

Fry the chicken fillets in hot melted butter until cooked through and golden brown. Keep them warm until required in a covered ovenproof dish in the oven at around 120°C.

You can either serve the fillets as they are with a sprinkling of freshly chopped coriander or with a satay sauce made from the reserved marinade - make a roux, add a glass of water and stir until it thickens, add the reserved marinade and simmer for 15 minutes, stirring often.

Check for taste and seasoning. Pour over the chicken fillets and sprinkle with freshly chopped coriander.

CHICKEN IN RED WINE
Serves 10

🍳 10 minutes
📟 1 hour

10 chicken legs
100ml vegetable oil
350g streaky bacon rashers, diced
5 garlic cloves, crushed
20oz/500g button mushrooms, cleaned
Large bouquet garni or 3 tsp mixed herbs
5 tbsp chopped fresh parsley

3oz/75g butter
10 button onions
Salt and pepper
1 bottle red wine (70-75cl)
10 tbsp seasoned flour
Small tin tomato purée (optional)

Coat the chicken legs in the seasoned flour placed in a shallow dish. In a mixture of butter and oil, fry the chicken legs in batches and keep warm in the oven in a large ovenproof dish.

In the same pan, fry the bacon until cooked, turning occasionally (about 5 minutes), then remove from the pan and keep warm with the chicken, evenly scattered over the dish. Still in the same pan (adding butter and oil if necessary), fry the seasoned onions gently until tender, adding the bouquet garni/herbs, mushrooms and garlic for the last 2-3 minutes.

Add the wine to the frying pan and boil for about 3 minutes, until it has reduced a little. If using tomato purée, stir it in then and cook, stirring, for another 1 minute until well incorporated. Pour the contents of the frying pan over the chicken and bacon in the ovenproof dish and bake at 180°C for 45 minutes.

If you need to keep this dish warm until ready to serve, simply turn down the temperature to about 120°C.

Check the seasoning. If too sharp, add a little sugar to the sauce, mix well and cook for another 10 minutes. Remove the bouquet garni if using. Serve with a generous helping of the sauce and parsley sprinkled over the top.

CHICKEN or TURKEY FILLETS IN A CREAMY MUSTARD SAUCE (GF)
Serves 10

🍳 5 minutes
📟 40 minutes

10 chicken or turkey fillets
2-3 tbsp Dijon mustard (according to taste)
3oz/75g butter

Salt and pepper
500ml single cream

In a large frying pan, fry the fillets until cooked through and golden brown. Place in a warm ovenproof dish to keep warm in the oven at 120°C.

Put the mustard in the frying pan on low heat and mix with the remaining butter. Add the cream and stir well to mix all the ingredients thoroughly.

Simmer for 1 minute, then pour over the chicken fillets and bake in the oven, covered, at 150°C for 20-30 minutes. You can continue to keep warm in the oven at 100°C until ready to serve.

COQ AU VIN BLANC
Serves 8

🔥 10 minutes
⏱ 1 hour

1 x 1¾kg chicken	5-6 tbsp butter
5oz/125g diced streaky bacon	12 button onions
10oz/250g quartered button mushrooms	1oz/25g flour
2 crushed garlic cloves	1 bouquet garni
1 bottle dry white wine (table wine is fine)	Salt and pepper
8oz/200g croûtons, brushed with melted butter and toasted	

Cut chicken into 8 pieces and reserve the liver. Season the pieces with salt and pepper. Melt 2 tbsp of the butter in a large casserole and brown the bacon and onions. In a separate pan, melt 2 tbsp butter and sauté the mushrooms.

When the bacon and onions are nicely browned, remove with a slotted spoon and reserve, and put the pieces of chicken into the same casserole.

Sauté the chicken pieces until golden. Sprinkle with the flour and let it brown a little, adding more butter if necessary. Add the garlic and the wine. Bring to a boil and then add the sautéed mushrooms, the reserved bacon and onion mixture, bouquet garni and salt and pepper.

Cover and simmer for 45 minutes. Remove the chicken, mushrooms, onions and bacon and keep them hot in a deep dish. Strain the sauce into a saucepan, taste for seasoning and place it over a low heat. Cover the pieces of chicken and vegetables with the velvety sauce and serve hot with croûtons.

22

DUCK BREASTS WITH RED WINE SAUCE (GF)
Serves 4

🔪 5 minutes
▯ 20 minutes

23

4 x 250-300g duck breasts, with skin left on
125ml/4 fl oz beef stock
125ml/4 fl oz red wine
1 tbsp chopped fresh rosemary

1 tsp lemon juice
½oz/15g butter
Salt and black pepper
1 tsp tomato purée

Marinade
5 garlic cloves, sliced
1 tbsp chopped fresh rosemary

2 tbsp balsamic vinegar

To make the marinade, combine the garlic, vinegar and rosemary in a bowl. Score the duck breasts and spread with the marinade, chill for 30 minutes.

Put the duck breasts, skin-side down, with the marinade in a frying pan and cook for 5-7 minutes. Turn and cook for a further 5 minutes. Remove from the pan and keep warm.

Spoon any excess fat from the frying pan. Add the stock and wine and bring to the boil. Cook over a high heat until reduced to a dark glaze, then add the tomato purée and lemon juice.

Remove from the heat and whisk in the butter, letting it thicken the sauce as it melts. Taste for seasoning.

Slice the duck breasts, and arrange on warmed serving plates. Spoon the sauce around the duck. Sprinkle with the chopped rosemary and serve at once.

DUCK BREASTS WITH A CRANBERRY AND ORANGE SAUCE (GF)
Serves 8-10

🔪 7 minutes
▯ 40 minutes

8-10 duck breasts with skin on
300-400ml of water
1 orange sliced in to 8-10 rounds
Dash of Port
Ground cinnamon

1 bag cranberries
3-4oz/75-100g caster sugar
Juice of 1 orange
100ml red wine

Pre-heat your oven to 200°C. Score the skin of the duck and rub in a little salt and sprinkle with a little cinnamon. In a hot frying pan, fry quickly on each side to seal in the juices.

Place the duck breasts on a baking tray, skin side up and place a slice of orange on top of each breast. Place in the oven and cook for 30-40 minutes - the breasts should be cooked until medium, so still quite red in the middle.

To make the sauce, place your cranberries in a saucepan and add the sugar, water, juice of the orange, Port and red wine. Bring slowly to the boil allowing the cranberries to burst and then simmer until the sauce takes on a thin syrupy consistency.

Thinly slice your duck breasts, fan out onto hot serving plates and spoon over the sauce.

LAMB CHOPS WITH TARRAGON SAUCE (GF)
Serves 10

 5 minutes
30 minutes

10 lamb chops	5 tbsp olive oil
18oz/450g onions, finely chopped	3 tbsp tarragon vinegar
375ml white wine	375ml double cream
750ml lamb or chicken stock	Salt and pepper
3 tsp chopped fresh tarragon	Tarragon sprigs to garnish

Heat 2½ tbsp oil in a frying pan and brown the chops in batches for 2 minutes on each side or until the fat is crisp.

Place the chops in a roasting tin and bake at 200°C for 15 minutes for medium-rare, 20 minutes for well-done.

Heat the remaining oil in the cleaned pan, add the onion and cook for 5-7 minutes until soft but not coloured. Add the vinegar and wine, bring to the boil and simmer for 2 minutes. Add the cream and stock, simmer for 10 minutes or until syrupy. Check the seasoning.

Add the chopped tarragon and roasting juices to the sauce. Warm through.

Serve the chops garnished with tarragon and accompanied by the sauce.

MOROCCAN LAMB (GF)
Serves 8-10

 10 minutes
2 hours 15 minutes

1.1kg/2.5lbs of diced lamb fillet, well trimmed	2 lamb stock cubes
1 tsp cinnamon and 1 cinnamon stick	1 tsp ground ginger
1 handful of dried apricots	1 large tin tomatoes
1 handful of prunes	1 bayleaf
1 onion, chopped	150ml/¼ pint red wine
1 tsp curry powder	300ml/½ pint water
1 tsp cardamom seeds (optional)	

Soften the onion in a little oil and add the lamb to seal it. Cover with the tomatoes, wine and add all the other ingredients except the dried fruit. Sprinkle in the stock cubes and pour in the water.

Simmer gently on the hob or put in a pre-heated oven at 160°C for 2 hours until the meat is tender; stirring occasionally. When the meat is nearly cooked (after 1¾ hours), stir in the apricots and prunes and cook for 15 minutes. Taste for seasoning.

ROSEMARY AND GARLIC ROAST LAMB (GF)

🍳 5 minutes
🔲 2 hours

Serves 10

2kg joint (leg, shoulder or rolled)
6 tbsp olive oil
6 garlic cloves, peeled and cut lengthways into thin pieces

2 tsp each salt and pepper
6 tsp rosemary

Place the meat in an ovenproof dish or roasting tin. In a bowl, prepare the rub by mixing together the oil, rosemary, salt and pepper.

With a thin sharp knife, cut slits all over the meat at 5 cm intervals. Push a piece of garlic into each slit as far as possible. Rub the rosemary mixture all over the joint. Bake in the oven at 170°C for the required time, basting occasionally.

Use some of the meat juices to make gravy. Serve mint sauce separately (see recipe on page 72).

LAMB WITH A ROSEMARY AND REDCURRANT SAUCE

🍳 5 minutes
🔲 35 minutes

Serves 8

16 lamb chops (2 each unless large)
1 medium jar (340g) of redcurrant jelly

Handful of fresh rosemary
½ chicken stock cube

Cook the lamb chops in the oven at 200°C for approx. 20-30 minutes.

To make the sauce, put the redcurrant jelly into a saucepan, dissolve the chicken stock cube in 100ml of water and add to the jelly.

Finely chop the rosemary, add to the saucepan and bring slowly to the boil.

When you are ready to serve, thicken the sauce by mixing a little flour with some oil in a cup and add to the sauce. Or you can use cornflour: which will slightly thicken your sauce.

Just before serving pour the sauce through a sieve to remove the rosemary and any bits of flour.

ROAST LEG OF LAMB WITH A PORT AND ROSEMARY GLAZE (GF)
Serves 4-6

🕐 5 minutes
⬜ 2 hours

1 whole leg of lamb
½ tbsp fresh chopped rosemary
1 tbsp olive oil
1 level tbsp cornflour (Maizena)

2 tbsp Port
2 garlic cloves, sliced
4 tbsp blackcurrant jelly
Black pepper

Pre-heat the oven to 190°C. Place the leg of lamb into a roasting tin, slit the fat and press in the garlic slices. Then brush with oil and season with grated black pepper. Place in the middle of the oven and cook for 20 minutes per 1lb and 20 minutes over.

Mix together the jelly, port and chopped rosemary and spoon over the lamb for the last 15 minutes of cooking. Pour the juices from the roasting tin into a saucepan, put fresh rosemary sprigs into the slits on the meat and return to the oven for the last 5 minutes.

Blend the cornflour with a little cold water, stir it into the meat juices and bring to the boil gently. Rest the meat for 10 minutes then carve and serve with the sauce.

LAMB CHOPS WITH GINGER AND CORIANDER (GF)
Serves 10

🕐 10 minutes
⬜ 10 minutes

12cm piece root ginger, peeled and chopped
5 tbsp chopped fresh coriander
5 tbsp freshly squeezed orange juice
2½ tsp Chinese five-spice powder
Salt and pepper
5 tbsp dry sherry

10 lamb chops
5 garlic cloves
5 tbsp thin runny honey
13oz/325g softened butter
5 tbsp white wine vinegar

Place the ginger and garlic in a food processor with the honey and orange juice. Process until finely chopped. Add the five-spice powder and softened butter, and process again until evenly mixed.

Season the chops with salt and pepper. Heat half the spiced butter in a frying pan. Add the chops and fry for 3-5 minutes on each side until tender and well browned. Transfer to a warmed plate and keep warm.

Add the remaining spiced butter, vinegar and sherry to the pan. Bring to the boil, then add the coriander.

Serve the chops immediately with the sauce.

ROAST LOIN OF PORK WITH PEACHES (GF)
Serves 6

🍳 5 minutes
🍴 1 hour

1 x 7-rib loin of pork
Salt and freshly ground black pepper
8 fresh peaches, halved and stoned (or 2 tins in natural juice)

8oz/200g butter
1 bunch of fresh thyme, chopped

Preheat the oven to 200°C. Score the skin of the pork about 1cm apart through the fat nearly to the meat. With a knife carefully part the meat from the ribs.

Mix the chopped thyme into the butter with the seasoning and rub a little of the butter into the gap you have made between the ribs and the meat.

Push in as many peaches as you can fit and pack the rest of the butter on top. To hold the meat and ribs together and hold the peaches in place, simply fasten some string around the pork loin in 3 or 4 places and tie firmly.

Place in a roasting tray with any leftover peaches and other vegetables you wish to cook with it - potatoes, parsnips, celeriac and Jerusalem artichokes are all good - and cook for 30 minutes per pound of weight of pork plus 30 minutes over.

Allow the meat to rest for 10 minutes before serving. If the vegetables are cooked beforehand, remove and keep warm. Make some gravy with the meat juices in the roasting tin at the end of cooking with a little boiled water and white wine.

PORK CHOPS or FILLETS IN APPLES AND CIDER (GF)
Serves 10

🍳 5 minutes
🍴 45 minutes

10 pork chops or fillets
5 apples, peeled and sliced
1 bottle medium cider
5 cloves garlic, crushed

3oz/75g butter
Salt and pepper
3 large onions, chopped
2 tsp Herbes de Provence

In a large frying pan, fry the seasoned chops until golden brown. Place in an ovenproof dish and keep warm in the oven.

In the same pan, fry the onion, garlic and herbs, seasoned with salt and pepper, until soft. Scatter these evenly over the chops. Cover with the apple slices. Pour the bottle of cider evenly over the dish.

Cover and bake in the oven at 180°C for 45 minutes (or a little more). The liquid should reduce during baking and can be used as thin gravy when serving.

PORK MEDALLIONS DIJONNAISE (GF)
Serves 4

🥄 5 minutes
📷 27 minutes

4 pork chops
4 shallots, peeled and finely chopped
150ml/¼ pint chicken stock
200ml tub of fromage frais or 150-200ml cream

1 tbsp oil
150ml/¼ pint white wine
1 tbsp Dijon mustard
1 tbsp fresh chopped parsley

Heat the oil in a large frying pan, place in the pork chops and cook on each side until lightly browned for 4-5 minutes, transfer to a preheated oven at 180°C and continue cooking for 15 minutes.

Stir the shallots into the frying pan that the meat was in and cook until softened. Pour over the wine and stock and simmer gently for 10 minutes or so. Stir in your fromage frais or cream and mustard, and heat through for 2 minutes. Remove the pork from the oven and serve with the sauce poured over each chop.

PORK CHOPS IN HONEY AND MUSTARD (GF)
Serves 10

🥄 5 minutes
📷 10 minutes

10 pork chops
5 tbsp clear honey
3oz/75g butter

Salt and pepper
3 tbsp Dijon mustard

Mix together the honey and mustard in a large bowl. Season the chops and coat each one completely with the honey-mustard mixture. Leave to marinate in the covered bowl in the fridge for a few hours (or from morning to evening).

In a large frying pan, fry the chops, trying to keep as much marinade on them as possible, until golden brown and cooked through. Serve immediately.

SWEET AND SPICY PINEAPPLE PORK (GF)
Serves 10

🍳 5 minutes
🔲 35 minutes

10 pork steaks
2 tbsp mild curry paste
4 tbsp mango chutney
800g canned pineapple pieces in natural juice

4 garlic cloves, crushed
4 tbsp lemon juice
Chopped parsley to garnish

Drain and roughly chop the pineapple pieces, reserving the juice.

Heat a non-stick frying pan and dry-fry the pork steaks over a high heat for 2 minutes each side until golden brown. Transfer to an ovenproof dish large enough to hold the pork steaks in one layer.

Add the garlic and curry paste to the pan. Fry gently for 30 seconds. Stir in the pineapple and juice, lemon juice and chutney. Bring to the boil and bubble to reduce slightly, then pour over the pork.

Bake at 200°C for about 25 minutes, basting occasionally. Serve garnished with the parsley.

LEMON BRAISED PORK CHOPS WITH CUMIN AND MUSHROOMS
Serves 10

🍳 5 minutes
🔲 55 minutes

10 pork chops
5 tsp ground cumin
Salt and pepper
5 onions, thinly sliced
1½ tsp sugar
24oz/600g (quartered) chestnut or brown cap mushrooms

5 tbsp plain flour
1½ tsp ground coriander
5 tbsp olive oil
750ml white wine
2½ lemons, thinly sliced

Sift the flour with the cumin, coriander, salt and pepper. Turn the chops in the spiced flour to coat.

Heat the oil in a frying pan, add the chops and fry until browned on both sides. Transfer to a plate.

Stir the onions into the fat remaining in the pan and cook gently for 10 minutes until soft and golden. Add the wine and sugar. Bring to the boil and boil briskly for about 5 minutes until reduced and slightly syrupy.

Lay the lemon slices over the base of an ovenproof dish. Cover with the onions and wine, then place the chops on top. Cover with foil and bake in the oven at 190°C for 20 minutes.

Uncover and add the mushrooms, pushing them into the gaps between the chops. Bake uncovered for a further 15 minutes. Serve immediately.

BOEUF BOURGUIGNON
Serves 8

 10 minutes
2 hours

8oz/200g lardons
1.8 kg/4 lb braising steak or topside
2oz/50g butter
60ml/4 tbsp oil
2 garlic cloves, crushed
Salt and pepper
Bouquet garni

300 ml/½ pint beef stock
600 ml/1pint red wine
24 shallots
4 tbsp plain flour
14oz/350g button mushrooms
Chopped parsley to garnish
1 tbsp tomato purée

Dice the bacon. Cut the meat into 4cm/1inch pieces. Heat half the butter and oil in a pan and fry the bacon for 5 minutes and drain. Fry the meat in batches for about 8 minutes until browned.

Put the bacon in a casserole dish with the garlic. Stir in the flour and add the seasoning, the bouquet garni, stock and wine. Bring to the boil then add the tomato purée, stirring continuously. Cover and cook at 170°C for 1½ hours.

Heat the remaining butter and oil in a frying pan and sauté the onions for 10 minutes until golden brown. Add the mushrooms and onions to the casserole dish. Cook for a further 30 minutes or until the meat is tender. Garnish with the parsley.

BEEF STROGANOFF
Serves 4-5

 5 minutes
10 minutes

450g fillet of beef or rump steak
2 onions, finely sliced
7oz/175g mushrooms, sliced
1 tbsp finely chopped Fresh parsley
Salt and black pepper

3oz/75g butter
150ml soured cream
2 tbsp brandy
1 tsp flour

Melt half the butter in a pan, add the onions and cook gently until they are tender and golden brown. Add the mushrooms and cook for 3-4 minutes.

Cut the beef into strips ¼ inch wide and toss in the flour.

Remove the onions and mushrooms from the pan with a draining spoon and keep on one side. Add the remaining butter to the pan and when it is hot, add the strips of beef and fry briskly for 3-4 minutes. Return the onions and mushrooms to the pan, mix well, add salt and black pepper and soured cream. Cook for 2-3 minutes, add the warmed brandy and 'flambé' it (set it on fire!). Pour into the serving dish and sprinkle with the parsley. Serve at once.

ROAST FILLET OF BEEF WITH CHILLI PEPPER BUTTER (GF)
Serves 10

🔪 15 minutes
🍳 30-35 minutes

2 kg piece fillet of beef
Salt and pepper
Chopped chives to garnish

Olive oil for basting
20 large garlic cloves, peeled

Flavoured Butter
2 tsp mild chilli powder or chilli sauce
12oz/400g unsalted butter, softened
7 tbsp freshly grated Parmesan cheese

2 red peppers
2 red chilli peppers

Trim the meat and tie at intervals with string to keep a good shape. Rub all over with olive oil, salt and pepper.

To make the flavoured butter, grill the red peppers and chilli peppers under a high heat until charred. Cover, cool slightly, then peel off the skins. Halve and deseed then purée in a food processor. Add the butter, chilli powder or sauce, Parmesan and plenty of pepper. Process until evenly blended. Turn onto clingfilm, shape into a log and chill for at least 1 hour until firm.

Place the meat in a roasting tin, tuck the garlic cloves around the meat and roast at 230°C for 25 minutes for medium rare. Leave to rest in a warm place for 10 minutes before carving.

To serve, cut 20 thick slices of chilli butter. Carve the meat into chunky slices, 2 per person, arrange on warm plates and set a slice of pepper butter on top of each one to melt. Garnish with the roasted garlic cloves and chives.

BEEF AND OLIVE CASSEROLE (GF)
Serves 4

🔪 15-20 minutes
🍳 1 hour 30 minutes

1½lb trimmed rump steak
6oz rindless lean bacon
4oz/100g black and green olives

6oz/150g rindless fat bacon
¼ pint red wine
3-4 sliced tomatoes

Marinade
3 tbsp cooking oil
2-3 sticks of celery in 2.5cm pieces
¼ pint red wine
Bunch of fresh herbs
A few peppercorns

1 sliced carrot
1 diced onion
¼ pint wine vinegar
1 crushed garlic clove
Salt and pepper

To make up the marinade, heat the oil and add the vegetables. Fry until brown, then add the remaining ingredients, bring to the boil and simmer for 15 minutes. Allow to cool. Cut the meat into thick chunks and cover with the marinade.

Fry the fat bacon to extract the fat, then remove from the pan. Fry the meat on both sides in the bacon fat and put it in a casserole. Dice the lean bacon and add to the casserole with the marinade, wine and olives. Cover with greased greaseproof paper, then with a lid, and cook in oven at 170°C for 1½-2 hours. Before serving, remove the excess fat and add the tomatoes.

MUSTARD ROAST BEEF WITH YORKSHIRE PUDDINGS

🕐 10 minutes
🍳 2 hours

Serves 10

2 kg beef joint
1½ tbsp mustard powder
6oz/150g plain flour
400ml milk
4 tbsp hot fat from the roast

1½ tbsp plain flour
Salt and pepper
¾ tsp salt
2 large eggs

Place the beef in a roasting tin, with the thickest part of the fat uppermost.

In a small bowl, mix the flour with the mustard powder and season with salt and pepper. Rub the mixture over the joint.

Position the roasting tin so that the joint is in the middle of the oven and roast at 230°C for 30 minutes. Baste the beef and lower the setting to 190°C. Bake for a further 1 hour approximately, basting occasionally.

Meanwhile, make the Yorkshire pudding batter. Sift the flour and salt into a bowl. Mix in half the milk then add the eggs and season with pepper. Beat until smooth, then whisk in the rest of the milk.

Place the beef on a carving dish, cover loosely with foil and leave to rest in a warm place while cooking the Yorkshire puddings and making the gravy. Increase the oven setting to 200°C.

Pour off about 4 tbsp fat from the roasting tin and use to grease 8-12 individual Yorkshire pudding tins. Heat in the oven for 5 minutes or until the fat is so hot that it is almost smoking. Pour the batter into the tins. Bake for 15-20 minutes, until well risen, golden and crisp.

BEEF IN BEER

🕐 10 minutes
🍳 2 hours

Serves 10

1.5kg lean stewing or braising beef
Salt and pepper
4 medium-size chopped onions
2 garlic cloves
450ml water

4 tbsp flour
3oz/75g butter
6 medium-size sliced carrots
1 small turnip (optional)
450ml beer

Cut the beef into 3cm cubes. Toss in flour seasoned with salt and pepper. Fry briskly in hot butter until well browned, turning all the time. Remove to a plate.

Add onions, carrots and turnip (if used) to the remaining butter in the pan. Fry for 7 minutes, until pale gold. Add the garlic, replace the meat, pour in the water and beer. Bring slowly to the boil. Lower the heat. Cover the pan. Simmer very gently for 1¾ to 2¼ hours, until the meat is tender, stirring occasionally.

BACON-WRAPPED TROUT WITH LEEK AND ALMOND SAUCE (GF)
Serves 10

 8 minutes
10 minutes

20 thin rashers smoked streaky bacon	10 small whole trout, gutted
3oz/75g butter	5 tbsp oil
3oz/75g toasted flaked almonds	Parsley sprigs to garnish

Sauce

2 small leeks (green part), thinly sliced	3oz/75g butter
5 garlic cloves, crushed	3oz/75g ground almonds
150ml ginger wine	120ml double cream
Salt and pepper	

Lightly score the fish once or twice on each side. Wrap two rashers of bacon around each fish, securing in place with wooden cocktail sticks.

Melt the butter with the oil in a frying pan. Add the trout and fry gently for 5 minutes until the bacon is crisp and golden. Turn and fry for a further 5 minutes or until cooked through. Scatter the flaked almonds over the trout.

To make the sauce, melt the butter in a saucepan, add the leeks and garlic, and fry for 5 minutes until the leeks are softened. Stir in the ground almonds and ginger wine and cook gently for 3 minutes. Stir in the cream and season with salt and pepper to taste.

Arrange the trout and almonds on warm plates and add a generous spoonful of the sauce. Serve immediately, garnished with parsley.

SOLE MEUNIERE
Serves 10

 5 minutes
10 minutes

5 tbsp seasoned flour	13oz/325g clarified butter
Juice of 2½ lemons	13oz/325g unsalted butter
3 tbsp chopped fresh parsley	20 lemon wedges
10 Dover or lemon soles, skinned and fins removed	

Coat the fish with the seasoned flour, shaking off excess. Transfer to a warm dish and keep warm.

Heat the clarified butter in 2 very large frying pans. When hot, add the fish. Fry gently for about 5 minutes. Turn the fish and cook for a further 5 minutes.

Melt the unsalted butter in a clean pan and heat until turning golden brown. Add the parsley and lemon juice, pour over the fish immediately. Serve at once with lemon wedges.

COCONUT FISH CURRY

Serves 10

🍳 10 minutes
▭ 20 minutes

1.8kg cod or haddock steaks
5 tbsp plain flour
6-8 green chilli peppers (optional)
5 garlic cloves, crushed
8 tbsp lime juice
1 litre canned coconut milk
5 tbsp chopped fresh mint
6cm fresh root ginger, peeled & finely chopped

Salt and pepper
190ml oil
575g onions, finely chopped
1½ tsp turmeric
5 tsp curry paste
5 tbsp chopped fresh coriander
Coriander leaves to garnish

Season the fish and dust lightly with the flour, shaking off excess. Heat 7 tbsp oil in a heavy-based pan and fry the fish steaks in batches over a high heat for about 1 minute on each side until browned. Remove and set aside.

Heat the remaining oil in the cleaned pan and fry the onions with the chilli peppers for about 10 minutes or until they begin to soften and turn golden. Add the ginger, garlic, turmeric and curry paste. Cook for a further 1 minute.

Stir in the coconut milk and herbs, then simmer gently over a medium heat for 10-15 minutes or until syrupy. Return the fish to the pan to cook through until it is opaque and flakes easily when tested with a fork. Add the lime juice and serve immediately, garnished with coriander leaves.

SPICY FISH IN WHITE WINE (GF)

Serves 10

🍳 5 minutes
▭ 25 minutes

4 cloves garlic, finely chopped
4 tbsp finely chopped fresh coriander
2 medium onions, finely chopped
4 tbsp finely chopped fresh parsley
2 tbsp finely chopped fresh basil
10 fish fillets/portions (any white fish or salmon)

1½ lemons, thinly sliced
1 tsp ground ginger
1 tsp Cayenne pepper
Salt and pepper
5 tbsp olive oil
75cl dry white wine

Pour the seasoned oil into an ovenproof dish large enough to hold the fish portions in one layer and coat all sides and base of the dish. Rinse the fish in cold water and dry well. Place the fish in the ovenproof dish and turn each portion over until it is completely coated with oil.

Sprinkle the garlic, onions, ginger, Cayenne pepper, parsley coriander, basil, salt and pepper evenly all over the fish. Place one lemon slice on each fish portion. Pour the wine into the dish last. Cover and bake in the oven at 200°C for 20-25 minutes.

If the juice has not reduced enough during cooking, reduce in a pan and pour over the fish to serve.

POACHED FISH WITH HOLLANDAISE SAUCE (GF)
Serves 10

 5 minutes
15 minutes

10 small fish/fish fillets	1 litre milk or broth
Hollandaise sauce (See page 71)	Salt and pepper
Optional flavouring to taste (herbs)	

In a shallow pan, heat the milk or broth, then add the seasoned fish and simmer very gently until just cooked. Timing varies according to size and thickness of fish. Test with a sharp pointed knife. Drain well and serve with a generous coating of Hollandaise sauce.

SKATE WITH CAPER SAUCE (GF)
Serves 10

 5 minutes
15 minutes

10 pieces of skate wing, skinned	5 shallots, roughly chopped
2½ celery sticks, cut into 10 pieces	5 bay leaves
3 tbsp black peppercorns	12 tbsp cider vinegar
5 tsp capers, chopped	425 ml double cream
5 tbsp chopped fresh parsley	Salt and pepper
Parsley sprigs to garnish	

Put the shallots, celery, bay leaves, black peppercorns and 10 tbsp of the cider vinegar into a large saucepan with about 3 litres of cold water. Slide in the skate and slowly bring to just below the boil - the surface should barely bubble. Cover the pan, lower the heat and cook gently for 7-10 minutes until the skate flesh just parts from the bones.

In the meantime, put the capers in a small pan with the cream, parsley and seasoning. Bring to the boil, lower the heat and simmer for 1 minute. Off the heat, stir in the remaining 2 tbsp vinegar. Check the seasoning.

Lift the skate from the poaching liquor onto warm serving plates. Spoon on the cream sauce and garnish with parsley sprigs. Serve immediately.

children's tea

I f there are younger children staying in your chalet, then you will usually be expected to provide an early children's tea at around 5.30pm.

Some children can be fussy and difficult to please, but it's important to their parents that they eat enough of the right food groups, and that they eat enough to replace the energy they burn during the day!

Some companies will provide you with a set children's menu that you are expected to stick to. If this has not been provided, it is best to have a range of children's meals that you can rustle up, and also to talk to guests on arrival regarding their children's likes and dislikes (within reason - you can't be expected to provide three completely different meals each night for three children, for example.)

The following simple meals offer an idea of the type of meals that are both nutritious and child friendly:

Spaghetti Bolognaise
Macaroni Cheese
Sausage and Mash
Homemade Chicken Nuggets (no Twizzlers here!)
Shepherds Pie
Chicken or Turkey Escalopes with a mushroom or tomato sauce
Breaded Fish with potato wedges

These dishes should be served with suitable vegetables.

A simple dessert should be provided, but you should always have yoghurts and fresh fruit available at the end of a children's meal.

Just to start you off, we've provided a simple recipe for Spaghetti Bolognaise.

SPAGHETTI BOLOGNAISE (GF)
Serves 4

5 minutes

20 minutes

1 lb of minced beef
1 small clove garlic, crushed
400g tin tomatoes

1 onion finely chopped
1 tbsp tomato puree
Salt and pepper

Sweat the onion in a casserole dish or saucepan until soft. Add the garlic and stir quickly round the pan. Add the minced beef and fry for 3-4 minutes until browned. Stir in the tomato puree and then add the tin of tomatoes and stir well. Season. Stir and cook for 20-30 minutes on the hob, just simmering or in the oven at 170°C.

Serve with pasta or with mashed potatoes piped on top. You can also add carrots, courgettes, sweetcorn and mushrooms to this recipe for added variety. However bear in mind that as you are cooking for children, do not over-season or make it spicy.

Vegetables

You may be wondering why we have devoted a whole chapter to vegetables - this is because, on a modern chalet holiday, the standards of catering required rise well above the historic stereotype of British plain boiled vegetables!

The vegetables are an important part of any meal, and should always complement it, in terms of both taste and colour.

They might both be as healthy, but think, for example, how much more visually rewarding a plate of chicken accompanied by sauteed French beans, honey glazed carrots and potato dauphinoise would be than with creamy potatoes, leeks and cauliflower!

Just as important is the actual cooking of the vegetables. Over or undercooked vegetables will spoil any meal, and over-cooking vegetables reduces their nutritional value.

In addition to the recipes in this chapter, you can also serve vegetables with some of the sauces found on pages 71-72, for example cauliflower cheese, or minted potatoes.

GRATIN DAUPHINOISE (GF)
Serves 4

🍳 10 minutes
🍽 15 minutes

18oz/450g potatoes
Salt and black pepper
Pinch of nutmeg

2 eggs
300ml hot milk
1oz/25g Gruyère cheese

Preheat the oven to 200°C. Scrub and peel the potatoes and slice them very thinly. Place the potatoes in a buttered ovenproof dish, season with salt, pepper and nutmeg between each layer.

Whisk the eggs lightly and add the hot milk. Place the mixture in a measuring jug and pour into the potato dish by making a small space at one side. Do not pour the mixture all over the top of the potatoes.

Slice the Gruyère cheese thinly and arrange this over the top. Cook for 50 minutes or until the potatoes are tender. Serve hot.

POMMES DE TERRE BOULANGERE (GF)

🍳 10 minutes
🍽 1 hour

3oz/75g cheese, grated
750g potatoes
3 onions, very thinly sliced
2oz/50g butter, melted
Chopped parsley

215ml white stock
3 tbsp white breadcrumbs
Salt and black pepper
Pinch of nutmeg

Preheat the oven to 190-200°C. Scrub and peel the potatoes and slice them very thinly. Arrange the potatoes and onions overlapping in the bottom of a buttered ovenproof dish. Sprinkle with some of the grated cheese and season lightly with salt and black pepper and nutmeg. Repeat these layers until the dish is full.

Pour over the stock and sprinkle with the breadcrumbs. Pour the melted butter over the breadcrumbs and cover with a piece of well buttered greaseproof paper. Cook for 50 minutes to 1 hour or until the potatoes and onions are tender. 15 minutes before serving, remove the paper to allow the top of the dish to brown. Clean the edges of the dish before serving and sprinkle the parsley over the potatoes. Serve hot.

ROAST POTATO WEDGES (GF)
Serves 10

🍳 5 minutes
🍽 45 minutes

1 kg medium size potatoes
Salt and pepper
½ tsp Cayenne pepper

6 tbsp vegetable oil
1 tsp garlic salt

Wash well, but do not peel the potatoes. Cut each potato lengthways into 4 wedges. In a baking tray, mix all the other ingredients. Place the wedges in the tray and toss them in the dressing until they are well coated.

Bake at 180°C for 45-55 minutes, until the wedges are brown and crisp, turning them occasionally. Drain and transfer to a warm serving dish.

SAUTÉED POTATOES (GF)
Serves 10

🍳 5 minutes
▢ 12 minutes

1kg potatoes, peeled and diced
2 garlic cloves, finely chopped
Salt and pepper/Cayenne pepper
2 tbsp oil

1 onion, chopped
2-3 tbsp chopped parsley
2oz/50g butter

Sweat off the chopped onions and garlic until soft in some of the oil. Add the potatoes along with the butter. Fry off for 10 minutes until golden. You may need to add extra oil or butter as the potatoes are very absorbent.

SAUTÉED FRENCH BEANS (GF)
Serves 10

🍳 5 minutes
▢ 20 minutes

1kg French beans
2 cloves garlic, finely chopped
2-3 tbsp fresh chopped parsley
1 medium size onion, chopped

Salt and pepper
2oz/50g butter
2 tbsp vegetable oil

If you are using fresh beans top and tail them, then boil in salted water to half cooked consistency. If you are using frozen beans, thaw them, but do not boil them first.

In a very large frying pan or wok, fry the onion gently until slightly soft. Add the beans, garlic, salt and pepper and fry on medium heat for about 15-20 minutes, stirring frequently, until the beans are soft and browning on the outside. Add most of the chopped parsley and fry for a further 1 minute.

Transfer to a warm serving dish. Sprinkle the remaining parsley over the beans.

GLAZED BABY CARROTS (GF)
Serves 4

🍳 3 minutes
▢ 7 minutes

½ oz/15g brown sugar
18oz/450g baby carrots or
9oz/225g normal carrots

1oz/25g butter
Salt and black pepper

Garnish
Finely chopped parsley

Scrub and top and tail the baby carrots if using. For larger carrots peel and cut them into batons. Place the carrots in a saucepan with the butter, sugar, salt and black pepper. Add enough cold water to almost cover the carrots.

Cook quickly until all the water has evaporated and carrots are just tender and lightly coated in butter. Place in a hot serving dish, sprinkle with the parsley and serve at once.

FRENCH STYLE PEAS (GF)

Serves 10

⏱ 2 minutes
🔲 10 minutes

800g fresh or frozen garden peas
3oz/75g butter
4 sprigs of mint

4 tbsp sugar
Salt and pepper

Place the peas in a saucepan. Boil a kettle of water and pour enough into the pan to cover the peas. Add ½ tsp salt, the sugar and the mint and simmer for 10-15 minutes until the peas are tender.

Drain well. Transfer to a warm serving dish. Toss in the butter. Sprinkle a little finely chopped mint over the peas to serve.

BAKED AUBERGINES (GF)

Serves 10

⏱ 5 minutes
🔲 30 minutes

3 large aubergines
2 garlic cloves, finely chopped
2 tsp Herbes de Provence

4 tbsp olive oil
1 large onion, finely chopped
Salt and pepper

In a mixing bowl, combine together the oil, garlic, onion, herbs, salt and pepper.

Clean and cut the aubergines into 2cm cubes (do not peel them). Transfer them to the mixing bowl and toss them in the mixture until they are well coated.

Pour into a greased, shallow oven-to-table dish and bake in the centre of the oven at 180°C for 20-30 minutes, tossing regularly, until the aubergines are soft and browned.

If the aubergines appear to get too dry during baking, add a little oil or boiling water to the dish and toss well.

CAULIFLOWER CHEESE

Serves 4-5

⏱ 10 minutes
🔲 15 minutes

1 cauliflower
300ml Béchamel sauce (see page 71 for recipe)
3oz/75g cheese, grated

Salt and black pepper
Brown or white breadcrumbs
1oz/25g butter

Remove the outside leaves from the cauliflower. Cut the cauliflower into small florets removing the thicker, harder stalk. Cook in a large saucepan of boiling salted water until just tender. Drain well and place in a hot serving dish.

Make the Béchamel sauce according to the recipe. Stir ¾ of the cheese into the Béchamel sauce and stir until it has melted. Taste, adjust the seasoning and pour over the cauliflower.

Mix the remaining cheese with the breadcrumbs and sprinkle over the cauliflower. Cut the butter into small pieces and sprinkle these over the top. Brown under a hot grill, or in the top of a hot oven, 220°C for a few minutes. Serve immediately.

SWEET AND SOUR RED CABBAGE (GF)
Serves 10

  5 minutes
1 hour

1 small red cabbage	2 medium-size red onions
Salt and pepper	2oz/50g butter
6 tbsp soft brown sugar	6 tbsp red wine vinegar

Melt the butter in a large saucepan. Fry the onions gently until soft. Stir in the finely shredded red cabbage. Stir in the brown sugar, vinegar, salt and pepper. Simmer for 1 hour or more, tasting occasionally and adjusting the seasoning if necessary. The cabbage is ready to serve when it has become softer and the sweet and sour taste has penetrated right through.

BUTTERED LEEKS (GF)
Serves 10

  3 minutes
15 minutes

1kg leeks	Salt and pepper
Small bunch of finely chopped chives	3oz/75g butter
Cream	

Trim and cut the leeks into 5cm pieces and wash thoroughly. Boil in salted water for about 15 minutes until the leeks are tender. Drain well and transfer to a warm serving dish. Add the butter, salt and pepper and most of the finely chopped chives and toss. Pour a little cream over the top, sprinkle the remainder of the chives and serve.

SWEET ROASTED FENNEL (GF)
Serves 4-6

5 minutes
55 minutes

700g fennel (about 3 bulbs)	1 lemon, halved
3 tbsp olive oil	2oz/50g melted butter
1 tsp caster sugar	Salt and pepper
2 large sprigs of fresh thyme	

Quarter the fennel lengthways and place, cut side up, in a roasting tin.

Squeeze the juice from the lemon halves over the fennel, then drizzle with the olive oil and melted butter. Add the empty lemon halves to the tin. Sprinkle with the sugar and season generously with salt and pepper. Add the thyme sprigs.

Cover with a dampened piece of non-stick baking parchment. Bake at 200°C for 30 minutes. Remove paper and bake for a further 20-30 minutes or until the fennel is tender and slightly charred.

Vegetarian and alternative diets

With increasing public awareness of food allergies, coupled with a greater desire for healthy eating, you will find yourself dealing with lots of different dietary requirements during your season.

All guests are asked about specific dietary requirements when booking, but during any season you can almost guarantee that you will find a few unexpected special needs on arrival. For this reason, it is best to be ready for vegetarians and vegans, and to always keep a stock of gluten free ingredients.

You should also check with the guests on arrival whether they have any specific requirements or preferences. You may find that some 'vegetarians' eat chicken or fish, so it's always worth asking.

Food allergies
Some food allergies can be more serious than others - for example some nut allergies can be very severe - in this case, you should avoid using the offending ingredient at all in the kitchen during that week, as even a trace can be potentially fatal.

Dairy, gluten or wheat free
The above intolerances are quite common now, and we have included a few recipes that cater for all of these. You will also find that many of our other recipes throughout the book are gluten free (marked GF). Guests are usually happy to give guidance on what they can and cannot eat.

Religious diets
Some religions have specific requirements regarding what may be eaten and how it may be prepared. Many guests in this situation will bring their own food.

NUT ROAST
Serves 6-8

🍳 15 minutes
⏲ 1 hour

11oz puff pastry	6oz chestnut purée
1 small onion	2 eggs
2 celery sticks	1 tsp paprika
2 cloves garlic	1 tsp oregano
1 tbsp oil	2 tbsp lemon juice
2oz button mushrooms	4oz walnuts
4oz pecans	Beaten egg to glaze
4oz Brazil nuts	Salt and pepper

Shell the nuts. Roll out the pastry, line a 2lb loaf tin leaving enough overlapping each side to cover the top. Peel, chop and fry the onion, celery, garlic in a little oil. Put in a bowl with all the other ingredients, except the mushrooms. Mix well and bind with the eggs.

Fill the tin half full with the mixture. Embed the mushrooms in the mixture, fill with the remaining mixture and press down. Brush the pastry edges with a little egg, cover the pie with the overlapping pastry. Trim the edges.

Put a baking sheet on top of the tin and turn over. Remove the loaf tin. Put a few cuts in the top of the pastry and brush lightly with the beaten egg.

Bake at 220°C for 30 minutes. Reduce the temperature to 180°C and cook for a further 30 minutes.

VEGETARIAN SPINACH ROULADE
Serves 6

🍳 10 minutes
⏲ 30-35 minutes

2-3 large spoonfuls of cream cheese	3 handfuls of spinach
1 good handful of grated cheddar cheese or Ricotta cheese	5-6 eggs
	Salt and black pepper

For the base

200-250g of any type of savoury biscuits, e.g. cheese biscuits	75-100g butter, melted

Crush the biscuits and mix with the melted butter, until the biscuits stick well together. Press into the bottom of an 8 inch loose ring tin. Mix all the filling together in a food processor and pour into the tin. Bake in the oven at 180°C until firm to the touch.

Place a handful of grated cheese on top of the flan and place back into the oven and cook for another 5-10 minutes until the cheese on the top has browned.

VEGETARIAN INDIAN CURRY
Serves 4

🍳 15 minutes
▦ 45 minutes

1 tbsp vegetable oil
1 onion, chopped
1 apple, chopped
1 tbsp medium-strength curry powder
250g cauliflower, in florets
175g mushrooms, sliced
600ml vegetable stock
30g sultanas
1 tbsp garam masala

2 garlic cloves, crushed
3 celery sticks
1 tsp ground ginger
125g French green beans
250g potatoes, in cubes
400g can drained chick peas
1 tbsp tomato purée
175g basmati rice

Salad
4 chopped tomatoes
1 green chilli, seeded and chopped finely
4 spring onions, trimmed and chopped

7cm chopped cucumber
1 tbsp fresh coriander

Mint Raita
150ml natural yoghurt
Fresh mint sprigs to garnish

1 tbsp chopped fresh mint

Heat the oil in a large saucepan and fry the garlic, onion, celery and apple gently for 3-4 minutes. Add the curry powder and ginger, and cook gently for 1 more minute. Add the remaining ingredients except the rice and garam masala. Bring to the boil, then reduce the heat. Cover and simmer for 35-40 minutes.

To make the salad, combine all the ingredients. Cover and chill. To make the raita, mix the yoghurt and mint together. Transfer to a serving dish, cover and chill.

Cook the rice in lightly salted, boiling water until just tender, according to instructions on the packet. Drain thoroughly. Just before serving, stir the garam masala into the curry. Divide between 4 warmed serving plates, and serve with the salad, mint raita and rice. Garnish the raita with fresh mint.

GRILLED POLENTA PILED WITH SLICED VEGETABLES
Serves 4-6

🍳 15 minutes
🔲 20 minutes

175g polenta
600ml boiling salted water
2 courgettes, halved and sliced lengthways
1 fennel bulb, trimmed and
quartered lengthways

150ml cold water
30g butter
1 red onion, thickly sliced
2 tomatoes, cored and sliced
Melted butter for brushing

Marinade
4 tbsp olive oil
3 garlic cloves
Salt and black pepper

2 tbsp red wine vinegar
2-3 tbsp chopped parsley

Put the polenta into a saucepan, cover with the measured cold water, and leave to stand for 5 minutes. Add the boiling salted water to the pan, return to the boil, and simmer for 10-15 minutes stirring, until smooth and thickened.

Sprinkle a baking tray with water. Stir the butter into the polenta, then spread the mixture over the baking tray in a 1cm (½ inch) layer. Leave to cool.

For the marinade combine the oil, vinegar, garlic, parsley and salt and pepper to taste. Add the courgettes, fennel, tomatoes, and onion. Cover and leave to marinate in the refrigerator for 30 minutes.

Lift the vegetables out of the marinade and cook on a very hot griddle pan for 4-5 minutes on each side. Cut the polenta into strips and cook on the griddle pan brushing with melted butter for 1-2 minutes on each side until golden. Pile the vegetables on top of the polenta and serve.

STUFFED PEPPERS WITH RICE AND CHEESE
Serves 4

🍳 15 minutes
🔲 15 minutes

225g freshly boiled rice (about 100g raw)
100g grated cheese
150ml fresh single cream
25g butter

4 medium size green peppers
½ tsp mustard
Salt and pepper

Cut the tops off the peppers. Remove seeds and cores. Put peppers into a saucepan. Cover with boiling salted water. Carefully lift them out of the pan. Stand them upside down to drain on soft kitchen paper.

Combine rice with cheese, mustard and cream. Season to taste with salt and pepper. Stand the peppers in a shallow heatproof dish. Fill with equal amounts of rice mixture. Put a knob of butter on top of each one. Completely cover dish with aluminium foil. Re-heat in the centre of the oven at 180°C for 15 minutes.

You could also use red peppers or courgettes instead of green peppers.

MUSHROOM, SPINACH AND ROASTED POTATO BAKE
Serves 6

🕓 15 minutes
🍳 1 hour 30 minutes

900g small potatoes, scrubbed
6 tbsp olive oil
25g dried porcini mushrooms (optional)
75g Parmesan cheese freshly grated
450g mixed mushrooms (shiitaki, brown cap)
400g large spinach leaves, trimmed
2 garlic cloves, crushed
5 tbsp sun-dried tomato paste
2 tsp chopped thyme

300ml white wine
300ml vegetable stock
300ml double cream
175g Gruyère cheese, grated
2 onions, peeled
Salt and black pepper
2 eggs, beaten
300ml Greek yoghurt
Herb sprigs to garnish

Quarter the potatoes and place in a large roasting tin. Drizzle with 4 tbsp oil and turn to coat. Roast at 200°C for 40 minutes or until tender and golden. Meanwhile, soak the dried porcini in warm water to cover (if using) for 15 minutes; drain and chop. Roughly chop the onions, mushrooms and spinach.

Heat the remaining oil in a large, heavy-based pan and gently fry the onions for 10 minutes or until soft. Add the fresh mushrooms and garlic; cool over a high heat for 5 minutes. Stir in the tomato paste, porcini if using, thyme and wine; simmer for 2 minutes. Add the stock and cream, bring to the boil and bubble for 20 minutes or until well reduced and syrupy.

Transfer to a 2.3 litre (4 pint) ovenproof dish. Stir in the potatoes, spinach and Gruyère and half the Parmesan. Season well. In a bowl, beat the eggs with the yoghurt and seasoning, pour over the vegetable mixture and top with the remaining Parmesan.

Bake at 200°C for 30-35 minutes, until golden and bubbling.

VEGETABLE BURGERS
Serves 4

🕓 10 minutes
🍳 10 minutes

200g leeks, finely chopped
200g grated carrots
2 tsp finely chopped fresh parsley
100g sweetcorn
100g breadcrumbs
50g butter

300g grated celeriac
200g grated potatoes
1 finely chopped onion
2 eggs
Salt and pepper
2 tbsp vegetable oil

Mix all ingredients together thoroughly, reserving a little parsley for sprinkling. Divide into 4 or 8 equal amounts, depending whether you wish to make large or small burgers. Shape into compact burgers.

In a large frying pan, heat the butter and oil together. Fry the burgers on a medium heat for about 5 minutes on each side, until cooked through and golden brown. Serve on a warm serving dish sprinkled with the reserved chopped parsley.

TURKEY OR CHICKEN RISOTTO
(Dairy, Gluten, Wheat and Egg Free)
Serves 4

🕐 10 minutes
▭ 30 minutes

2 tbsp vegetable oil
50g mushrooms, halved or quartered
350ml water or chicken stock
75 g fresh or frozen French beans,
sliced finely

1 leek, chopped roughly
250g brown rice
1 tbsp of raisins
175g cooked turkey or chicken
Salt and pepper

Heat the oil in a saucepan, add the leek and fry gently until it is just beginning to soften. Add the mushrooms and cook for 2 minutes. Add the rice, stir for 1-2 minutes, then add the water or stock. Stir well, then bring to the boil and simmer, uncovered for 15-20 minutes or until the rice is cooked and all the liquid has been absorbed (if all the liquid is absorbed before the rice is done, add a little more).

If you are using fresh beans, blanch them briefly in boiling water. Add the beans to the risotto along with the raisins. Cut the turkey or chicken into small pieces, stir it into the risotto and cook for a few minutes to heat through, then season to taste and serve. This risotto is good either hot or cold.

MUSHROOM AND NUT RISOTTO (Vegetarian, Dairy, Gluten, Wheat and Egg Free)
Serves 4

🕐 10 minutes
▭ 30 minutes

2 tbsp olive, nut or vegetable oil
1 celery stick, finely chopped
1 head of chicory, finely chopped
250g large flat mushroom, finely chopped
50g walnuts or cashew nuts, chopped
Salt and pepper

1 small onion, finely chopped
175g brown rice
150ml dry white wine
150ml water
Juice of ½ - 1 lemon

Heat the oil in a wide pan and gently fry the onion, celery and chicory until they are beginning to brown.

Raise the heat, add the mushrooms and cook for several minutes. Add the rice, cook for 1-2 minutes, then stir in the wine and water.

Reduce the heat, cover and simmer for about 20 minutes or until the liquid has been absorbed and the rice is cooked. Add extra water if the liquid is absorbed too quickly.

Add lemon juice to taste and season with salt and pepper. Just before serving, stir in the nuts.

BACON AND CABBAGE CASSEROLE
(Dairy, Gluten, Wheat and Egg Free)
Serves 4

☕ 10 minutes
🍲 30 minutes

250g bacon, chopped quite finely	1 large onion, finely chopped
500g green or Savoy cabbage, sliced thinly	4 tbsp oil
1 large cooking apple, peeled, cored and chopped	Salt and pepper
200ml red wine or vegetable stock	125g large flat mushrooms, sliced

Put the bacon and onion in a large pan with 1 tbsp of the oil and fry them until the bacon has started to crisp and the onion to brown. Add the cabbage, apple and red wine or vegetable stock to the pan, stir well. Cover and cook gently for 15 minutes.

In a separate pan, cook the mushrooms briskly in the remaining oil, then add them to the cabbage mixture. Continue to cook, covered, for 15 minutes. The cabbage should be just cooked but still slightly crisp. Season to taste and serve as a main dish or as an accompaniment to roast meat.

PINEAPPLE CHICKEN (Dairy, Gluten, Wheat and Egg Free)
Serves 4

☕ 5 minutes
🍲 45 minutes

1 large onion, sliced thinly in rings	4 chicken joints
1 tbsp fresh rosemary	1 tsp salt
A pinch each of black pepper and paprika	½ tsp ground ginger
400ml unsweetened pineapple juice	

Preheat the oven to 180°C. Place the chicken joints in an ovenproof dish and sprinkle over the onion rings, rosemary, salt, ginger, pepper and paprika. Pour over the pineapple juice and bake uncovered, for about 45 minutes or until the chicken is cooked through and brown on the top. Serve with brown rice.

POTATO, LEEK AND APPLE PIE (Vegetarian, Dairy, Gluten, Wheat and Egg Free)
Serves 4

☕ 10 minutes
🍲 40 minutes

1 large cooking apple, peeled, cored and sliced	2 tbsp olive oil
1kg potatoes, sliced thickly	2 leeks, sliced thickly
375g white cabbage, sliced finely	3 tbsp sesame seeds (optional)
Salt and pepper	

Preheat the oven to 180°C. Steam the potato slices until half cooked. Pour the oil into a large ovenproof dish and arrange half the potatoes in the bottom. Mix together the sliced leeks, cabbage and apples, season lightly with salt and pepper and arrange over the potatoes. Cover with the remaining potatoes and add water to the dish to the depth of about 1cm.

Sprinkle the sesame seeds over the potatoes, if used, and bake for 30-40 minutes or until the potatoes are cooked and the seeds are nicely browned.

desserts

While it's obviously a good thing for guests to keep their sugar levels up while on a skiing holiday, it's not necessarily a good thing to serve them heavy or stodgy puddings.

It's best to offer a variety throughout the week, consisting of a mixture of fruit-based desserts, with perhaps one chocolate-based dessert and one caramel-based dessert.

It's best to prepare your desserts in the morning where possible, leaving you more time in the evening to concentrate on food that can't be cooked in advance.

In terms of presentation, you can be quite creative with desserts, using cream, fruit, coulis, chocolate sauce, icing sugar, mint leaves and many more. Explore your creative side and experiment in the early stages of your season!

MASCARPONE AND LIME CHEESECAKE
Serves 6-8

🕒 15 minutes
▭ n/a

200g pack of ginger biscuits, crushed
2 x 250g tubs Mascarpone cheese
Finely grated zest and juice of 2 limes

50g butter, melted
40g icing sugar, sifted

To Decorate
50g deluxe dark chocolate

50g caster sugar

Mix together the crushed biscuits and melted butter. Press into the base of a lightly greased 7-8 inch loose bottom tin, then refrigerate.

Put the Mascarpone, icing sugar, lime zest and juice in a bowl and beat together well. Pour over the base and chill for 2 hours before serving.

Decorate with chocolate curls or chocolate leaves.

TIRAMISU
Serves 8-10

🕒 20 minutes
▭ n/a

4 x 250g cartons of Mascarpone cheese
250ml coffee flavoured liqueur (e.g.Tia Maria)
425ml very strong black coffee
Cocoa powder for sprinkling

40g caster sugar
3 eggs, separated
About 30 sponge fingers

Put the Mascarpone, sugar and egg yolks in a bowl and beat with an electric mixer until evenly blended and creamy.

Whisk the egg whites in a clean bowl until standing in stiff peaks. Fold into the Mascarpone mixture until evenly incorporated. Spoon a quarter of this mixture into the base of a glass serving bowl.

Mix liqueur and coffee together in a shallow dish (a breakfast bowl is ideal as you can use the rim to drain the dipped biscuits). One at a time, dip one third of the sponge fingers in this mixture for 10-15 seconds, turning once, drain excess liquid, then place on top of the Mascarpone mixture in the serving bowl, in a single layer to cover it.

Cover the sponge fingers with one third of the remaining mixture, then dip another one third of the sponge fingers in the coffee mixture and layer them as before. Repeat with another layer of Mascarpone and sponge fingers.

Spread the remaining Mascarpone mixture over the top and swirl with a palette knife. Sift cocoa powder liberally all over the top.

Cover the bowl and chill in the fridge for 24 hours (or at least from the morning until the evening) to allow flavours to develop before serving.

BREAD AND BUTTER PUDDING
Serves 6

15 minutes
45 minutes

750ml (1¼ pint) milk	50g caster sugar
Finely grated rind of 1 lemon	2 tbsp brandy
65g butter	½ tsp rosewater
6 thick slices of white bread	1 tbsp Demerara sugar
50g no-soak dried apricots	1 tsp ground cinnamon
50g sultanas	3 eggs
50g currants	

Heat the milk in a saucepan with the grated lemon rind to the boil. Turn off the heat and leave to infuse for 20 minutes. Meanwhile, butter the slices of bread and cut into triangles. Roughly chop the apricots. Mix together the sultanas, currants and apricots. Place three quarters of the mixed fruit in the base of a 1.4 litre (2½ pint) shallow ovenproof dish. Arrange the bread neatly overlapping on top of the mixed fruit, with the points uppermost, then sprinkle on the remaining fruit.

Beat together the eggs, caster sugar, brandy, rosewater and flavoured milk. Spoon the mixture over the bread and leave to soak for 5 minutes. Gently push the bread down into the custard.

Dust the top with Demerara sugar and cinnamon. Place in a roasting tin containing enough hot water to come halfway up the side of the dish. Bake at 180°C for about 50-55 minutes or until the custard is lightly set and the top is golden brown.

CRÈME BRÛLÉE
Serves 6

10 minutes
50 minutes

1 tbsp caster sugar	4 egg yolks
2 x 284ml (10 fl oz) cartons double cream	Few drops of vanilla essence

To Finish
50g (2oz) caster sugar

Beat the egg yolks and sugar together. Warm the cream very slowly in a heavy-based saucepan. Carefully stir in the egg mixture. Continue cooking gently, stirring constantly, until thickened enough to coat the back of a spoon. Add the vanilla essence.

Strain into six ramekin dishes and place in a roasting pan, containing 1 inch of water. Place in a preheated cool oven at 140°C for 30-40 minutes, until the pudding is set. Remove the dishes from the pan and cool, then place in the refrigerator.

To finish sprinkle evenly with sugar. Place under a preheated hot grill until the sugar has caramelised, or caramelise with a blowtorch.

Cool and chill in the fridge for 2 hours before serving.

PEARS COOKED IN RED WINE WITH CHOCOLATE SAUCE

🕐 5 minutes
🍳 35 minutes

Serves 10

10 round, slightly under ripe pears	Juice of 2 oranges
1½ to 2 litres red wine (to cover pears in pan)	6 tbsp sugar
Rind of 1 orange (peeled from the orange)	3 cloves (optional)
1 tsp cinnamon or 1 cinnamon stick	10 leafy mint sprigs

Chocolate Sauce
200g dark chocolate in pieces   150ml double cream

In a large pan or pot, heat the wine with the orange juice, rind, sugar, cinnamon and cloves. In the meantime, peel the pears whole, leaving the cores and stalks in place. Cut the base of each pear straight so that it stands freely. Stand the pears in the wine and cook them on low heat for up to ½ hour, until tender.

Make the chocolate sauce just before serving. Put the chocolate pieces in a gently simmering Bain Marie and pour into it the cream which you have just boiled in a saucepan. Stir until the chocolate and cream are thoroughly mixed. Simmer gently and stir often until ready to serve.

Put each hot pear into a small dessert bowl or sundae cup with a small 'puddle' of the cooking wine at its base. Coat each pear completely with a thin coat of chocolate sauce. Decorate each pear with a leafy mint sprig.

APPLE CRUMBLE

🕐 10 minutes
🍳 30 minutes

Serves 6

Crumble Topping

75g flour	75g soft brown sugar
50g ground almonds	50g unsalted butter

Filling

900g eating apples	50g unsalted butter
50g caster sugar	50g raisins or sultanas
A sprinkling of cinnamon	

To make the crumble topping, sift the flour into a mixing bowl, stir in the sugar and ground almonds, then work in the butter using your fingertips to make a very crumbly mixture.

Peel and core the apples and cut them into 2.5 cm chunks. Melt the butter in a large frying pan, add the apples with the sugar and cook over a high heat for 3 to 5 minutes stirring continually, until they are golden brown and tender. Transfer to a 1.7 litre pie dish. Scatter the raisins or sultanas on the top and sprinkle with cinnamon.

Spoon the crumble topping over the top and bake in the centre of the oven at 190°C for 25 minutes until the topping is golden brown. Serve warm with custard, crème anglaise, cream or ice cream.

Note: Instead of apples, other seasonal fruit (e.g. pears) or canned fruit (e.g. apricots) can be used.

cook in large ramekins ?

FRENCH APPLE TART
Serves 8

🔪 15 minutes
▢ 30 minutes

2 rolls of puff pastry
2 tbsp brown sugar
5 tbsp apricot jam

10 large apples
2 tsp cornflour

Preheat the oven to 190°C. Line a baking sheet or tray with lightly oiled greaseproof paper or non-stick parchment.

Place one roll of the pastry onto the prepared baking parchment. With the second roll of pastry, lay it onto a flat surface and cut all the way around the edge with a sharp knife, 2-2.5cm in from the edge. This will give you a thin round of pastry, which is placed over the top of the pastry base. Moisten the round and place on the base to form a border and press down lightly to seal.

Peel, core and roughly chop five of the apples. Place into a saucepan, with the sugar and heat slowly until the apples turn into a soft purée. Mix the cornflour with a little water to slake it and stir into the apple purée, leave to cool.

Meanwhile, halve, core and peel the remaining five apples. Slice them thinly and rub a little lemon juice over them to stop them discolouring.

Once the apple purée is cooled spread evenly over the pastry base, but not on the raised border. Then take your sliced apples and arrange on the top of the purée slightly overlapping each apple slice, working from the edge of the pastry base to the centre.

Place in the preheated oven and cook for 20-30 minutes, until the apples on the top are just soft and the pastry edge has risen and turned golden brown; the edges of the sliced apple should start to burn slightly. Leave to cool completely.

Just before serving prepare the glaze. Place the apricot jam in a small pan and melt over a low heat, brush over the apples to glaze.

RICH CHOCOLATE MOUSSE
Serves 4

🔪 15 minutes
▢ n/a

3oz/75g plain chocolate, broken into pieces
2 tbsp sherry
Chocolate curls to decorate

3 eggs, separated
3 tbsp whipped cream

Melt the chocolate in a bowl over a pan of hot water, then add the egg yolks and sherry and mix well. Whisk the egg whites until fairly stiff, then carefully fold into the chocolate mixture.

Divide between four ramekin dishes and leave in the refrigerator to set.

Pipe a cream rosette on each mousse and top with chocolate curls to serve.

afternoon tea

This is an important part of the chalet routine - guests love returning from the slopes and tucking into large slices of home made cake!

Afternoon tea should usually be laid out before you leave the chalet for the day. Each employer will have their own policy but it will usually consist of either a homemade cake or biscuits, plus bread, jams, honey and butter.

Coffee machines should be ready to switch on, kettle filled, teapot at the ready with teabags available, and enough cups, plates and knives for all of your guests.

Don't be tempted to buy a cake or biscuits if you're running out of time - guests expect home-baked, and will know if it isn't!

Two other tips to bear in mind are that cakes bake differently depending on the altitude and the oven they are cooked in, so it may take a few trials before your mum's favourite Victoria Sandwich recipe turns out as expected!

All of the recipes found in this chapter, however, are tried and tested, and will work at altitude.

We have included the yoghurt cake, a firm favourite with all experienced chalet staff! The great thing about this option is that it always works, the ingredients are easily measured (using the yoghurt pot), and the recipe can be used with many different flavours and toppings

Cakes can be topped or filled with melted chocolate, jam, cream, slices of lemon/lime, dusted icing sugar, and various icings that can be found on page 78.

(USE INGHAMS BOOK)

YOGHURT CAKE

Serves 12

🥄 5 minutes
📷 40 minutes

2 small tubs plain or flavoured yoghurt
2 tubs sunflower oil
3 tsp baking powder

2 tubs sugar
6 tubs plain flour
8 eggs

Pour the mixture into a 25cm greased circular tin or 2 sandwich tins and bake at 180°C for 45 minutes or until a skewer pricked into the centre of the cake comes out clean.

Decorate with coloured/flavoured plain icing. If making a sandwich cake, fill with jam, chocolate spread or butter cream filling (see recipe on page 78).

CARROT CAKE

🥄 10 minutes
📷 1 hour

150ml sunflower oil
225g self-raising flour
150g light muscovado sugar
100g carrots, grated
Walnut halves to decorate

2 tsp baking powder
50g walnuts, chopped
2 ripe bananas, mashed
2 eggs

Topping
175g full-fat soft cheese
100g icing sugar, sifted

50g soft margarine
A few drops of vanilla essence

Preheat the oven to 180°C. Grease and line an 8 inch deep round cake tin with greaseproof paper.

Measure all the ingredients for the cake into a large bowl and mix well until thoroughly blended and smooth. Turn into the prepared tin and level the surface.

Bake in the preheated oven for about 50-60 minutes until the cake is well risen and shrinking away from the sides of the tin. Allow to cool in the tin for a few minutes before turning out and leaving to cool completely on a wire rack.

For the topping, measure all the ingredients, except the walnuts into a bowl, or into a food processor, and mix well until smooth. Spread over the top of the cake, swirling the top with a spatula for a decorative effect. Decorate the top with the walnut halves. Chill a little before serving, and store in the fridge, as the topping is soft.

ALMOND CAKE
Serves 10

 10 minutes
🔲 40 minutes

200g butter
3 eggs
2 tsp baking powder
1 tsp almond essence
Butter cream filling (See recipe on page)
with ½ tsp of almond essence

200g caster sugar
150g plain flour
100g ground almonds
50g flaked almonds to decorate
Plain icing with a few drops of
almond essence

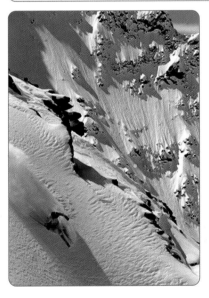

Cream the butter and sugar until creamy and light. Beat in the whole eggs, one at a time, adding a little sifted flour with each. Fold in the remaining flour/baking powder mixture and finally the ground almonds and almond essence.

Transfer the mixture to 2 greased sandwich tins and bake at 180°C for about 30 minutes, until well risen, golden brown and firm.

Leave in tins for a few minutes, then turn out onto a wire rack to cool.

In the meantime, prepare the butter cream filling and use to fill the centre of the cake when the cake is cold.

Make the icing and spread over the top of the cake. Place the flaked almonds on top immediately, in a single layer, and press them in gently to fix them to the icing.

CHOCOLATE CAKE

 10 minutes
🔲 40 minutes

150g self-raising flour
175g margarine
75g drinking chocolate, NOT cocoa powder
3tbsp boiling water

175g caster sugar
3 eggs

This is the ultimate, rich, indulgent chocolate cake.

Grease and line 2 shallow 8 inch cake tins. Place all the ingredients in a food processor and beat well together for 3-4 minutes. Add the boiling water a little at a time, not all may be necessary.

Pour into the prepared tins and bake at 160°C for 40 minutes, until the cake has peeled away from the sides and is springy to the touch. Leave to cool for a while and turn out onto a wire rack.

BANANA FRUIT TEA LOAF

🍳 10 minutes
📟 1 hour 30 minutes

¾ level tsp mixed spice
100g butter
100g caster sugar
2 eggs, beaten
2 large bananas
50g glacé cherries, chopped

100g sultanas
50g walnuts, chopped
225g flour
2 tsp baking powder
½ level tsp salt

To Finish
100g icing sugar, sifted

4 tbsp lemon juice

Preheat the oven to 180°C. Grease and line a 2lb loaf tin. Cream the butter and sugar together until light and fluffy, add the eggs a little at a time beating well between each addition. Peel the bananas and mash up in a bowl using a fork. Stir into the mixture with the fruits and chopped walnuts.

Sift the flour, baking powder and mixed spice together and carefully fold into the mixture. Pour into the prepared tin, smooth the top and bake for 1 hour. Reduce the oven temperature to 160°C, and bake for a further 30 minutes. (This may not be necessary, check cake after first hour). Cool in the tin for approximately 10 minutes, then place on a wire rack until completely cold.

To finish, mix the lemon juice with the sifted icing sugar to give a coating consistency and pour over the top of the cake. Leave to set. The cake may be served plain or sliced and lightly buttered.

DATE AND WALNUT LOAF
Serves 10

🍳 10 minutes
📟 45 minutes

250g plain flour
1½ tsp mixed spice
150g caster sugar
3 eggs
75g walnut pieces
A little plain icing

2 tsp baking powder
150g butter
1 tsp finely grated lemon rind
100g chopped dates
A few walnut halves

Cream the butter and sugar until creamy. Beat in alternately 1 egg and sifted flour/baking powder/mixed spice mixture until these ingredients have been used up. Mix in the remaining ingredients.

Bake in a greased loaf tin at 180°C for 45 minutes or until cooked through (insert skewer into cake - if it comes out clear, then it is cooked through)

When cold, decorate the top with plain icing and a few walnut halves.

ICED LIME TRAY BAKE
Makes 9 squares

🍽 5 minutes
🔲 45 minutes

175g soft margarine
250g self-raising flour
3 eggs
Grated zest of 2 limes

175g caster sugar
1½ tsp baking powder
3 tbsp milk

Icing
250g icing sugar

Juice of 2 limes

Lightly grease a 9x12 inch cake tin and line the bottom with baking parchment. Combine all the cake ingredients in a large bowl and beat well for about 2 minutes until smooth and thoroughly blended. Turn into the prepared tin and level the surface. Bake in a preheated oven at 180°C for 35-40 minutes until the cake is well risen, springy to the touch, and beginning to shrink away from the sides of the cake tin. Leave to cool slightly in the tin, then turn out on to a wire rack, peel off the lining paper and cool.

For the icing, sift the icing sugar into a bowl. Mix in enough of the lime juice to give a slightly runny consistency. Pour over the cooled cake, spreading carefully with a palette knife, and leave to set. Cut into squares and serve.

CHOCOLATE BROWNIES

🍽 10 minutes
🔲 35 minutes

3oz self-raising flour
4oz chocolate, melted
6oz soft brown sugar
2oz chopped walnuts

3oz butter, melted
2 eggs, beaten

Melt the chocolate and the butter together slowly in a saucepan. Mix in the sugar and stir in the eggs a bit at a time and add the flour and beat well until smooth. Mix in the walnuts. Pour into a baking tray lined with bakewell paper. Cook at 180°C for 30-35 minutes. The top should be just hard, but the middle still slightly gooey.

COCONUT AND PINEAPPLE CAKE
Serves 12

🍽 5 minutes
🔲 40 minutes

As for yoghurt cake, but with pineapple flavoured yoghurt
200 g grated coconut, reserve a little for decorating
1 can pineapple pieces, well drained, reserve the juice, reserve a few pieces for decorating

Mix all ingredients as for the yoghurt cake, then add the pineapple pieces and coconut and mix in well. Bake as for the yoghurt cake. When cold, make icing by mixing a little of the reserved pineapple juice and icing sugar, ensuring the icing is not too runny. Spread over the top of the cake. Immediately sprinkle the remaining coconut over the icing, press slightly to fix it. Use the reserved pineapple pieces to finish decorating the top of the cake.

useful extras

This chapter is brimming with added extras, including recipes for special occasions, regional specialities, and other essentials including pastry, sweet and savoury sauces, icing, drinks and cocktails.

Regional specialities
Always check with your employer first, but it can be a nice touch to offer a weekly regional speciality to your guests, for example a Savoyarde evening, where you might serve a cheese fondue.

Although the fondue is filling enough in itself, you could serve a platter of local cold meats to start or as an accompaniment.

Drinks and cocktails
Wine is usually served over dinner, but some chalet companies serve pre-dinner drinks along with canapés. The Kir and Kir Royale recipes are perfect for this.

Vin chaud/glühwein is an excellent way to welcome your guests into the chalet on arrival day, and creates a fantastic aroma of spices throughout the chalet. This will set your week off on a good footing!

ROAST TURKEY WITH STUFFING
Serves 10-12

🍳 15 minutes
⬜ 3-4 hours

1 quantity stuffing of your choice
4.5-5.5kg (10-12lb) oven-ready turkey
4-5 slices of streaky bacon

50g butter
Salt and pepper

Prepare the chosen stuffing. Spoon the stuffing into the neck end of the turkey only and place the bird in a large roasting pan. Calculate the cooking time of the turkey and pre-heat your oven to 180°C.

Cut the butter into small squares and place on top of the turkey. Sprinkle well with salt and ground black pepper. Place the bacon on top of the breast of the turkey horizontally. Cover the bird with a large piece of strong aluminium foil. Place into the oven and roast.

About 30-40 minutes before the end of the estimated cooking time remove the foil, baste well with the pan juices and return to the oven for the rest of the cooking time. The turkey should be a rich, dark brown colour. Test the thickest part of the leg with a fine skewer or knife; the juices should run clear when the bird is cooked.

Lift from the roasting pan and place onto a serving dish and leave to stand for 15-20 minutes before carving. This allows the meat to relax and the juices to run back into the bird to keep it tender. Loosely cover with foil if desired. Use the pan juices to make a gravy.

CHESTNUT STUFFING

🍳 10 minutes
⬜ 25-30 minutes

435g tin unsweetened chestnut purée
200g peeled whole chestnuts
200g fresh breadcrumbs
75g smoked streaky bacon, chopped
2 eggs

175g shallots
75g butter
40g parsley chopped
Fresh grated nutmeg

Peel and finely chop the shallots. Melt the butter in a heavy-based pan and cook with bacon for about 10 minutes on a low-ish heat or until soft and beginning to colour.

Beat the eggs and add to the chestnut purée to help slacken it, or it will be hard to mix everything together later. Roughly chop the chestnuts and add them to the eggy purée, along with the breadcrumbs, parsley and buttery shallots and bacon. Add salt and pepper and a good grating of nutmeg. Use as required.

SAGE AND ONION STUFFING

🍳 10 minutes
▢ 20 minutes

1½oz butter
½lb onions
8-10 sage leaves
4oz fresh crumbs
1 large apple, peeled, cored & diced
Cider, or stock if necessary

1 egg
Salt and pepper
Grated rind of ½ a lemon
Squeeze of lemon juice

Chop the onions, put into a pan with cold water to cover well, bring to the boil and simmer for 4-5 minutes. Drain and squeeze out the excess liquid.

Pour a small quantity of boiling water on the sage leaves and stand for 5 minutes. Drain, dry and chop finely.

Put the crumbs into a bowl with the onions, sage, and apple and season highly. Beat the egg and stir in with the melted butter and lemon rind and juice. If the mixture is too dry, add a spoonful or two of cider or stock to make it blend nicely.

CHRISTMAS CAKE

🍳 20 minutes
▢ 3 hours 30 minutes

Grated rind of 1 orange
10oz plain flour
8oz butter
7oz brown moist sugar
4 large eggs
2oz almonds, chopped
4oz glace cherries
2 tbsp brandy, rum or sherry
1-1.5lbs dried fruit

1 tbsp black treacle
¼ tsp nutmeg
¼ tsp cinnamon
¼ tsp mixed spice
¼ tsp bicarbonate of soda
½ tsp salt
2-4oz mixed peel

Prepare a 9 inch/23cm cake tin by lining with a double thickness of greased paper.

Place the butter and sugar and grated rinds in a bowl and beat until light and fluffy. Add the treacle and beat for a few seconds.

Beat the eggs together and add slowly to the mixture beating continuously. Sift the flour with the salt, spices and soda and add gradually to the mixture beating all the time until it thickens. Gently fold in the fruit - if you are using a magimix it is best to do this by hand or the blades will break up the fruit too much.

Pour into the tin, level the top and place into a pre-heated oven at 150°C for 1 hour then slightly reduce the heat to 140°C for 2¼ hours. If the top begins to brown too quickly cover with tin foil. The cake is cooked when a sharp knife comes out clean.

Remove from the oven and leave to cool in the tin. When it is cold, remove from the tin, turn upside down and pour on the brandy, rum or sherry. When this has soaked in turn the cake the right way up, wrap in greaseproof paper and place in an airtight container.

Cover with marzipan and royal icing.

SIMNEL CAKE

🥄 15 minutes
🍳 3 hours

150g moist brown sugar
250g almond paste
100g currants
50g mixed cut peel
Grated rind and juice of 1 small orange
100g plain flour
3 eggs

200g sultanas
100g raisins
50g glacé cherries, halved
100g self raising flour
1 tsp ground cinnamon
150g softened butter

Decoration
1 egg, separated
150g icing sugar
Easter chick
1 metre 7.5cm wide gold lace ribbon

1 tsp water
1 tsp glycerine
Small Easter eggs

Line base and side of an 18cm round cake tin. Measure round the tin with a piece of string and cut to the exact size. Reserve the string.

Roll out half of the almond paste to a circle the size of the cake tin.

Mix together the sultanas, currants, raisins, mixed peel, cherries and orange rind and juice in a large bowl. Turn the fruit to coat in orange juice. Sift the flours and cinnamon into another bowl. Add the eggs, butter and sugar and mix until well blended. Beat for 1-2 minutes or until the mixture is smooth and glossy. Add the fruit mixture and mix well.

Spread half the cake mixture into the tin and level the surface. Put the circle of almond paste on top, then cover with the remaining cake mixture.

Bake for about 3 hours at 160°C, or until the cake begins to shrink from the side of the tin. It should spring back when pressed with the fingers.

Meanwhile, cut the remaining almond paste into three. Roll each piece to a long roll the length of the piece of string. Plait the rolls together.

Beat the egg yolk with the water. Arrange the plait around the edge of the cake top and brush with the egg yolk mixture. Cover the centre of the cake with foil if it is brown enough. Return the cake to the oven for 10 minutes or until the plait is browned. Leave the cake to cool in the tin.

To decorate, make Royal icing with the egg white, icing sugar and glycerine. Pour into the centre of the cake and leave to set.

Decorate with chicken and eggs, and fit the ribbon around the cake.

SHORTCRUST

 10 minutes
10-20 minutes

50g lard
225g plain flour
Pinch of salt

50g butter
8 tsp water, approx

Plain flour is used, and a proportion of half fat to flour. Water is generally used for mixing, though if a softer pastry is required milk may be used in its place. Lard does not have to be used, just increase the quantity of butter to 100g.

Sift the flour and salt into a mixing bowl.

Cut the fat into small pieces, add to the flour and rub in with the fingertips until the mixture resembles fine breadcrumbs.

Make a well in the centre, add the water and mix to a firm dough. Use as required. The pastry can be kept in the refrigerator for up to 2-3 days wrapped well in clingfilm and brought to room temperature before use.

PUFF PASTRY
Makes 450 g

 10 minutes
10-20 minutes

450g strong plain white flour
450g chilled butter
1 tbsp lemon juice

Pinch of salt
300ml chilled water

Sift the flour and salt together into a bowl. Cut off 50g of the butter and flatten the remaining large block with a rolling pin to a slab about 2cm thick. Set aside.

Cut the 50g butter into small pieces and rub into the flour with your fingertips.

Using a round-bladed knife, stir in enough water and the lemon juice to make a soft, elastic dough.

Turn out onto a lightly floured work surface and quickly knead the dough until smooth. Cut a cross through half of the depth, then open out to form a star.

Roll out, keeping the centre four times as thick as the flaps. Place the slab of butter in the centre of the dough. Fold the flaps over the dough, envelope-style.

Press gently with the rolling pin and roll out to a rectangle measuring 40x20 cm.

Fold the bottom third up and the top third down, keeping the edges straight. Wrap in clingfilm and leave to rest in the fridge for 30 minutes.

Put the pastry on a lightly floured work surface with the folded edges to the sides. Repeat the rolling, folding and resting sequence five times.

Shape the puff pastry as required, then rest in the fridge for about 30 minutes before baking.

CHOUX PASTRY

🍳 10 minutes
📟 10-20 minutes

150ml water
50g plain flour
25g butter

1 egg yolk
1 egg, beaten

Sift the flour onto a piece of greaseproof paper. Put the butter and water in a medium sized saucepan and warm until the butter has melted.

> This is used for éclairs, cream buns etc. and is made by an entirely different method.

Bring to the boil very slowly, shoot all the flour in at once and beat quickly - keep the pan over the heat for 1 minute if necessary - until the mixture thickens to a smooth glossy paste which leaves the sides of the saucepan. Add the egg yolk, beat well and gradually add the egg, beating continuously. The mixture should be thick and shiny. Use as required.

PÂTE SUCRÉE

🍳 10 minutes
📟 10-20 minutes

2 egg yolks
250g plain flour
50g caster sugar

75g butter

Sift the flour onto a board or work surface, make a well in the centre and add the sugar, butter and egg yolk. Work with the fingertips so that the butter and egg yolks are first rubbed into the flour and sugar and then worked together to form a ball of dough - the dough must be smooth and pliable, not at all crumbly.

> This is a crisp, short, sweet and melting pastry and is used for flans and tartlets and forms the basis of certain pâtisseries.

Wrap the dough and chill for 20-30 minutes. Use as required. Warm to room temperature before rolling out to fill your flan case.

RICH SHORTCRUST

🍳 10 minutes
📟 10-20 minutes

1 tbsp water, approx
225g plain flour
Pinch of salt
25g caster sugar

150g butter
1 egg yolk

Sift the flour and salt into a mixing bowl, stir in the sugar.

Cut the butter into small pieces, add to the flour and rub in with the fingertips until the mixture resembles fine breadcrumbs.

Make a well in the centre, add the egg yolk and water and mix to a firm dough. Use as required.

> This is used for flans, tartlets, and fruit pies when a richer pastry is needed, and particularly if the dish is to be eaten cold. Normally two-thirds of fat to flour is used, but no lard. An egg yolk or beaten egg is used to enrich and bind the pastry.

70

BÉCHAMEL SAUCE
Makes 300ml (½ pint)

5 minutes
5 minutes

300ml milk	15g butter
15g plain flour	Salt and white pepper

To make the roux, melt the butter in a saucepan. Stir in the flour and cook, stirring for 1 minute - it should look like wet sand. Do not allow it to burn on the bottom of the saucepan.

Remove from the heat and gradually pour the milk on to the roux a little at a time, whisking constantly. Keep going until all the milk is added. The pan may be returned to the heat when there is more liquid in the pan.

The sauce should be brought slowly to the boil, whisking constantly until the sauce has thickened and is smooth. Simmer for 2-3 minutes.

HOLLANDAISE SAUCE

5 minutes
5 minutes

1 small bay leaf	
3 tbsp white wine vinegar	2 egg yolks
75-100g butter at room temperature	6 peppercorns
Salt	

Place the vinegar, peppercorns and bay leaf in a small pan and boil rapidly until reduced to only 10ml (2 tsp); strain. Soften the butter until it is creamy.

In a small heatproof bowl, whisk the egg yolks with a pinch of salt and the flavoured vinegar until thoroughly combined. Set the bowl over a pan of gently simmering water on a low heat and whisk for about 3 minutes, until the mixture is thick enough to leave a trail when the whisk is lifted. Gradually add the butter, a little at a time, whisking constantly. When 75g has been added, season lightly with salt. If still too sharp, add a little more butter. The sauce should be lightly piquant and have a smooth pouring consistency. If too thick, add a little water or vinegar. Serve warm.

BREAD SAUCE

5 minutes
5 minutes

½ pt milk	
3-4 heaped tbsp fresh white breadcrumbs	2 cloves
1 onion	15g butter
1 bay leaf	Salt and pepper

Stick the cloves into the onion and put it with the bay leaf and milk into a saucepan. Cover and set on a very low heat to infuse for at least 10 minutes, or until the milk is well flavoured. Remove the onion and bay leaf; bring to the boil, and shake in the breadcrumbs.

Simmer for 3-4 minutes until thick and creamy, remove from the heat, season, stir in the butter. Reheat gently and use at one.

This sauce should be neither sloppy nor stodgy, and the necessary adjustments of crumbs or liquid must be made to produce the right creamy consistency.

MINT SAUCE

🔪 5 minutes
🍳 n/a

2-3 fl oz hot water
1 large handful of fresh mint leaves
2 tbsp sugar

2-3 fl oz vinegar

Finely chop the mint leaves, put into a bowl with the sugar, and add the hot water. When the sugar is dissolved add the vinegar. Leave to infuse for an hour or two before serving.

FRENCH SALAD DRESSING

🔪 5 minutes
🍳 n/a

6 tbsp olive oil
2 tbsp white wine vinegar
Pinch of sugar
Salt and black pepper

¼ tsp Dijon mustard
1 tsp chopped fresh herbs

Place all the ingredients in a small bowl and whisk until blended. Alternatively, place everything into screw top jam jar and shake well to mix.

AIOLI (GARLIC MAYONNAISE)

Makes 300 ml (for mayonnaise only, leave out the garlic!)

🔪 5 minutes
🍳 n/a

2 tsp lemon juice or white wine vinegar
1 tsp Dijon mustard
Salt and pepper
300ml light olive oil

2 egg yolks
4 crushed garlic cloves
Pinch of sugar

Place all the ingredients except the oil in a food processor and blend briefly until pale and creamy. With the blade motor running, pour in the oil through the feeder tube, in a steady stream, until the mayonnaise is thick. Thin to the required consistency, if necessary, with a little hot water.

Store in a screw-topped jar in the fridge for up to 3 days.

BARBECUE SAUCE

Serves 10

🔪 5 minutes
🍳 20 minutes

125g butter
3 tsp tomato purée
5 tsp mustard powder
Salt and pepper

3 medium onions, chopped
5 tbsp wine vinegar
5 tbsp Worcester sauce
425ml water

Melt the butter in a pan, add the onions and sauté gently for 10 minutes until softened. Stir in the tomato purée and cook, stirring, for 2 minutes.

Mix the wine vinegar, mustard, Worcester sauce, salt and pepper together in a bowl, stir in the water and add to the pan. Bring to the boil and let bubble for 10 minutes.

BLUE CHEESE DIP (GF)

5 minutes
n/a

Juice of a lemon
200ml soured cream
8oz/200g strong blue cheese
Few sprigs of chopped fresh chives

1 large garlic clove, crushed
Salt and pepper

Put all the ingredients in a food processor or blender and work to a smooth paste. Transfer to a serving dish and chill until required. Check the seasoning, sprinkle with chives and serve with a selection of crudités.

GUACAMOLE (GF)

5 minutes
n/a

6 ripe tomatoes, skinned, deseeded and chopped
3 large ripe avocados
6 tbsp crème fraîche
3 garlic cloves, crushed
2 red chilli peppers deseeded and finely chopped (optional)

6 tbsp lemon juice
1 tsp Tabasco sauce
1 tsp Worcester sauce
Salt and pepper

Halve, stone and peel the avocados, reserving the stones. Mash the avocado flesh in a bowl with the lemon juice and crème fraîche, then stir in the chopped tomatoes, chilli peppers, garlic, Tabasco and Worcester sauces. Season generously with salt and pepper.

Turn into a serving bowl and push the avocado stones into the mixture. Cover and refrigerate until ready to serve. Remove the avocado stones from the guacamole. Serve with crudités and tortilla chips or pitta bread.

TZATZIKI (GF)

5 minutes
n/a

2-3 tbsp finely chopped mint
1 large cucumber
500ml plain yoghurt
2 cloves of garlic, crushed

1-2 tsp lemon juice
Salt (optional)
Sprigs of mint to garnish

If the cucumber skin is tough or bitter, peel it off. If the seeds are mature, remove them. Grate the cucumber coarsely and put it in a sieve set over a bowl. Leave to drain for 30 minutes.

Line a second sieve with a piece of absorbent kitchen paper, set it over a bowl, pour in the yoghurt and leave to drain for 30 minutes.

Using your hands, squeeze out as much moisture as possible from the cucumber, then turn it into a clean bowl. Carefully transfer the yoghurt to the bowl of cucumber, peeling off the kitchen paper.

Blend the garlic and mint into the cucumber and yoghurt, then have a taste. Add a little lemon juice to sharpen it if necessary and a few pinches of salt. Cover and refrigerate until required (tzatziki is best eaten the day it is made). Just before serving, reblend the mixture and pour into a bowl. Garnish with a few sprigs of mint or a few slices of lemon.

BUTTERSCOTCH SAUCE
Serves 10

🍳 5 minutes
🔲 5 minutes

90g soft light brown (muscovado) sugar
60g caster sugar
150ml double cream
Juice of 1 lemon

60g butter
175g golden syrup
A few drops vanilla essence

Melt the butter, sugar and syrup together in a medium heavy-based pan over a low heat. Cook gently, stirring, for 5 minutes.

Off the heat, slowly stir in the cream. Add the vanilla essence and lemon juice. Stir for 1-2 minutes. Serve hot or cold.

CHOCOLATE FUDGE SAUCE
Serves 10-12

🍳 5 minutes
🔲 5 minutes

75g plain chocolate
6 tbsp warm milk
5 tbsp golden syrup

50g butter
300g soft brown sugar
1½ tsp vanilla essence

Break up the chocolate. Put it into a basin standing over a saucepan of hot water. Add the butter. Leave until the chocolate and butter have melted, stirring once or twice.

Blend in the milk. Transfer to a saucepan. Add the sugar and golden syrup.

Stand over a low heat. Stir until the sugar has dissolved. Bring to the boil. Boil steadily without stirring for 5 minutes.

Remove from the heat. Add the vanilla and mix well. Serve hot.

RASPBERRY COULIS
Serves 10

🍳 5 minutes
🔲 n/a

60ml Kirsch or Framboise liqueur
Icing sugar to taste

450g raspberries

Place the raspberries in a blender or food processor with the liqueur and work to a purée.

Pass through a sieve to remove the pips and sweeten with icing sugar to taste. Serve over ice cream or meringue.

BRANDY BUTTER
Serves 10-12

⏱ 5 minutes
🍳 n/a

225g unsalted butter
100ml approx brandy

200g granulated sugar

This makes a crunchy brandy butter that melts deliciously over Christmas pudding and mince pies.

Place the butter and sugar into a magimix or bowl and beat well together for 3-4 minutes, until the mixture is well combined and soft.

Slowly dribble the brandy into the mixture while beating continuously. This must be done slowly or the butter will curdle. Less or more brandy can be added according to taste.

Place into serving bowls and refrigerate before use, it will go hard. Remove from the fridge for 10 minutes before serving.

QUICK CUSTARD
Makes 1 litre

⏱ 5 minutes
🍳 5 minutes

2 heaped tbsp cornflour
1 litre milk
2 egg yolks

3 heaped tbsp caster sugar
½ tsp vanilla essence

Mix together the cornflour and sugar in a cup. Gradually stir in enough milk to dissolve the powder thoroughly (about half a cup). Boil the remaining milk in a saucepan. Remove from the heat as it comes up in the pan. Pour in the cornflour mixture while stirring. Continue to stir for 1 minute. The mixture thickens.

In a large Pyrex bowl, beat the egg yolks. Pour the mixture from the pan into the bowl, stirring constantly. The custard will thicken.

Place the bowl over a pan partly filled with a little boiling water. Continue to stir for 2-3 minutes or until the custard has reached the required consistency. Finally, stir in the vanilla essence.

CARAMEL SAUCE
Serves 10-12

⏱ 5 minutes
🍳 10 minutes

100 g caster sugar

300ml double cream

Melt the sugar in a small heavy-based pan over a low heat until liquid and golden. Cook over a medium heat until a dark caramel is formed.

Off the heat, immediately add the cream in a slow, steady stream, taking care as the hot caramel will cause the cream to boil up in the pan.

Stir over a gentle heat until the caramel has melted and the sauce is smooth. Serve hot or cold.

FONDUE SAVOYARDE (CHEESE)
Serves 6

🍴 10 minutes
🍳 10 minutes

Emmental cheese	1 garlic clove, crushed
Gruyère cheese	2 tsp cornflour
Reblochon cheese	3 tbsp Kirsch
200ml dry white wine	1 tbsp lemon juice
Pepper	Cubes of French bread

Chop the cheese into cubes.

Blend the cornflour to a smooth paste with the Kirsch.

Put the garlic, wine, lemon juice and the cheeses into a large saucepan with the blended cornflour. Bring slowly to the boil stirring all the time.

Simmer gently for 3-4 minutes, stirring all the time to stop it sticking to the bottom of the saucepan, season with pepper.

When ready to eat, transfer the cheese fondue to the fondue saucepan and place on the burner on the table.

Serve with plenty of bite sized chunks of slightly stale French bread.

Good accompaniments to the fondue are baked potatoes, green salad, bean salad, tomato salad and a selection of cold meats e.g. salami and Parma ham.

The great French invention!! A very easy meal to do and the clients usually love it. An easy pudding to go with this is sorbet, as it's a nice, light, palate cleanser after all the cheese. If your chalet has a fondue set, make sure you have enough methylated spirit/burning gel for the burners.

At the cheese counter in the supermarket, simply ask for cheeses for a fondue for the number of people you have and they will give you the right cheeses in the right amounts, so it's even easier!

TARTIFLETTE
Serves 10

🍴 5 minutes
🍳 30 minutes

1 large Reblochon cheese	1kg potatoes
A little butter to grease the dish	Salt and pepper

Grease an ovenproof dish. Cut the potatoes into thin slices, arrange them in the dish, season with salt and pepper. Place the Reblochon cut into two halves thicknessways on top of the potatoes, crusty side down.

Bake in the oven at 200°C for 30 minutes.

Serve hot with a green salad and dry Savoie white wine.

BEEF GOULASH
Serves 10

🥄 15 minutes
🍲 2 hours

1.8kg stewing steak, cut into chunks	Salt and pepper
3 tbsp plain white flour	5 tbsp oil
1.2kg onions, chopped	3 tsp dried mixed herbs
4 garlic cloves, crushed	7 tbsp paprika
700g canned plum tomatoes, peeled	500ml beef stock
Chopped fresh parsley to garnish	250ml soured cream
400g pancetta or thick cut rindless streaky bacon, cut into cubes	

Toss the beef in seasoned flour to coat.

Heat 2 tbsp oil in a deep flameproof casserole. Add the onions and fry gently for 5-7 minutes until starting to soften and turn golden. Remove. Add the pancetta to the pan and fry over a high heat until crispy. Remove. Heat the remaining oil in the pan and quickly fry the meat in small batches until browned on all sides.

Return the onions and pancetta to the casserole. Stir in the garlic and paprika. Cook, stirring, for 1 minute.

Add the herbs, tomatoes and stock. Bring to a simmer. Cover tightly and cook in the oven at 170°C for 1½ to 2 hours or until tender. Check after 1 hour, adding a little extra liquid if necessary.

Check the seasoning, then stir in the soured cream. Garnish with parsley and serve with noodles.

VEAL SCHNITZEL
Serves 10

🥄 10 minutes
🍲 4 minutes

10 veal escalopes	525g dried breadcrumbs
325g ground almonds	Salt and pepper
4 tbsp plain flour	3 beaten eggs
225ml oil	Lemon wedges to garnish

Lay the veal escalopes between two pieces of greaseproof paper and beat with a rolling pin to flatten them.

Mix together the breadcrumbs and ground almonds on a plate. Season the veal, then coat lightly with flour. Dip each piece in beaten egg, then into the breadcrumb mixture to coat, patting to help it adhere.

Heat 2 tbsp oil in a heavy-based frying pan. Fry the veal in batches for 1-2 minutes each side until deep golden brown, wiping out the pan and using fresh oil for each batch. Serve at once with lemon wedges.

BUTTER CREAM FILLING
Makes 350g (12oz) will fill and
cover a 7-inch cake

⏱ **5 minutes**
▢ **n/a**

125g butter, softened
225g icing sugar, sifted

Few drops of vanilla essence
1-2 tbsp milk

Cream the butter until soft. Gradually beat in the icing sugar, adding the vanilla essence and milk; to form a smooth icing.

Variations
Orange or lemon buttercream: Omit the vanilla and add a little finely grated orange or lemon rind and a little of the juice, beating well to avoid curdling the mixture.

Coffee buttercream: Omit the vanilla and milk. Add 2 tsp instant coffee powder dissolved in 1-2 tbsp hot water; cool before adding.

Chocolate buttercream: Flavour by adding 25-40g melted chocolate, omitting the 1 tbsp of the milk.

PLAIN ICING (FOR TOPPING TEA CAKES)
Makes enough to cover a 7-inch cake

⏱ **5 minutes**
▢ **n/a**

6 tbsp icing sugar

1-2 tsp cold water

Put the icing sugar in a small bowl, add the water and stir until well mixed and creamy. It is easy to adjust the consistency of the icing by adding a very small amount of water or icing sugar. This icing must not be too runny or it will spread where it is not wanted.

For your icing to complement your cakes better, use fruit juices instead of water to flavour/colour them, add cocoa powder to make a chocolate icing, also add essences or strong black coffee, to obtain different flavours.

APRICOT GLAZE
Makes enough to cover a 7-inch cake

⏱ **5 minutes**
▢ **n/a**

3 tbsp apricot jam

Heat the jam gently in a small saucepan until it 'melts'. Remove from the heat and brush generously over the top of a cake or fruit tart.

KIR
Serves 10

📖 5 minutes
🔲 n/a

2 bottles white wine, chilled

150-200ml Crème de Cassis
(blackcurrant liqueur)

Pour a little liqueur into each champagne or wine glass. Top with white wine.

KIR ROYALE
Serves 10

📖 5 minutes
🔲 n/a

150-200 ml Crème de Cassis liqueur

2 bottles Champagne or
sparkling white wine (chilled)

Pour a little liqueur into each champagne or wine glass.

Top with Champagne or sparkling wine.

Note: With both Kir recipes, do not be too generous with the liqueur as it is very sweet, and not to everyone's liking.

VIN CHAUD/GLÜHWEIN/MULLED WINE
Serves 10

📖 5 minutes
🔲 30 minutes

2 bottles red wine
2 cinnamon sticks
6 tbsp sugar

1 orange pricked with cloves
1 cup orange juice
4 tbsp Grand Marnier liqueur

Put all the ingredients into a large cooking pot, cutting the orange into quarters and squeezing them gently before placing them in the pot.

Heat gently, but do not allow to boil. Serve hot.

While some tour operators are happy to employ candidates with good home cooking experience, most employers prefer you to have some previous catering experience in a professional environment.

If you haven't worked in a kitchen, a cookery course is an excellent way to increase your chances of successful employment, and also to ensure you are going into the position with the necessary skills and experience.

Due to increasing demand for high quality chalet staff, Natives started its own courses specific to chalet cookery in 2002.

Guaranteed job if you pass!

These courses have been very successful and over 100 students have gone on to work in chalets around the Alps. The Natives course is widely recognised in the industry, not just because it produces good cooks, but specifically because it produces good chalet hosts.

We are so confident in our course that we are able to **guarantee** that we will find successful students a job.

You can find out more details about the courses and a details of possible employers over the next few pages.

the natives chalet cookery course

The Natives Chalet Cookery Course is widely recognised by both tour operators and smaller, private chalet companies, and offers a guarantee of successful job placement to all candidates who pass the course (*see below).

The five-day course is excellent value for money, and is taught by experienced seasonnaires, all of whom have run chalets previously. The course consists of a mixture of practical and theory sessions, offering specialist knowledge that will help you to run your chalet efficiently.

Course content

Main course sessions consist of a demonstration followed by a practical session where students work in pairs to try different recipes. Course tutors offer practical coaching throughout, followed by a tasting session and a group discussion.

Other short specialist sessions focus on key areas, including cakes, canapés, starters, soups, children's meals, vegetables and special diets.

Knowledge sessions are theory based, and cover other key aspects of running a chalet, including menu planning, presentation, safety and hygiene in the kitchen, time saving and budget saving tips, accounting/budgeting, shopping and guest management.

Assessment

Candidates are assessed throughout the course, and are given continuous feedback on performance so that strengths can be utilised and areas of weakness improved upon.

Course dates and location

Courses run throughout the months of July and August, with additional courses in May and October. The location of the course is St. Teresa's School for Girls, in the picturesque and rural setting of Effingham, Surrey.

How do I book a place?

Demand for the courses is usually very high, and courses are usually full by June. For further information, or to book a place on a course, please ring us on 08700 463377, or complete an enquiry form online at www.natives.co.uk/skijobs/cookery

*Job placement guarantee only applies to candidates age 21 and over holding an EU passport. However, to date, every student that has wanted a chalet job, regardless of age, has found one.

Thomson

Creating a warm glow

Catering - Ski Resorts

With your proven flair for catering and your passion for quality customer service, you're in your element whether you're cooking for up to 30 guests, designing the next day's menu or organising the rotas within a large and busy kitchen team.

You don't need to be an experienced or even a newly qualified Chef, although we're looking for these, we're also looking for people with more general skills and talent in catering who would suit our Chalet Host roles. We're inviting you to help make our ski holidays just as memorable as they can be. And, alongside our Chefs and Catering staff, we're always looking for great Hotel Managers, Assistant Managers, Hotel Hosts and Porters too.

After all, our customers have never been used to second best. Crystal Holidays aren't the UK's number one ski and snowboard specialists by accident. And Thomson summer and winter holidays are also known for providing the very best resorts and the very best teams that make every day so very special.

Let's talk about your talent and all the exciting places it could take you. Please call 0845 055 0258 for an application form or email overseasrecruitment@s-h-g.co.uk or apply online at www.shgjobs.co.uk quoting ref: NCCB7/05.

Carve a different future

Cut it with us

Discover a new and exciting career by joining us as a member of our Ski Resort Team. First Choice Ski is one of the UK's leading winter sports tour operators and is recruiting for a variety of positions for the upcoming ski season. You will need to have lots of enthusiasm with a flexible approach, aged 18 or over with excellent communication skills and the ability to think on your feet.

For more information on our positions, please visit **www.firstchoice4jobs.co.uk** to download an application form or alternatively contact us on **0870 750 1204** where we will be happy to answer any queries you may have.

 **First Choice**

ABTA
No. V1549

Equity SKI

Snow...work...play...Snow...work

Equity Ski are one of the UK's leading independent Tour Operators specializing in all-in ski holidays to Austria, France, Switzerland and Italy. Each season, we carefully select, train and look after around 170 staff who work in our hotels, chalets and resorts.

Positions include:

- Chalet Hosts
- Resort Representatives
- Ski Companions
- Hotel Managers
- Duty Managers
- Head Chefs
- Sous Chefs
- Kitchen porter/Night porters
- Senior Bar Staff
- Waiting/Housekeepers
- General Assistants
- Maintenance People

Recruitment for the winter season starts in June and continues once the season is under way so it's never too late to complete an application...

Visit www.equity.co.uk/employment
E mail recruitment@equity.co.uk
Call +44 (0)1273 886 911

the ingredients for your season

1069 eggs

764 tomatoes

42kg of cheese

1 snowmole guide

the little extras

If you really want to do the best possible job you can during your winter, you need to do more than just cook meals for your guest. Here are a few ideas for how you can get the most out of your season.

Welcome speech

Your employer may have specific guidelines on this, but you should always give a 'briefing' to your guests, usually on the evening of their arrival.

This doesn't need to be formal, but it is important as it should cover everything your guests might need to know in the chalet, for example meal times, chalet day off, après ski options, fire exits, honesty bar or packed lunch service. You can also offer to book a restaurant for chalet day off, unless your Rep/Resort Manager normally does this.

The 'Wow' Factor

Some extras take very little time, but will make your guests realise that you are making a real effort for them (and you never know, may help with tips at the end of the week!). For example:

- Pack your guests off with homemade scones on day one
- If you have a birthday in your chalet, go the extra mile by making and decorating a special cake, including candles
- Offer a wake up call - but be sure not to forget!
- Do a special afternoon tea, pre-dinner cocktail, or dessert on the last day

Weather forecast

Guests always want to know the weather forecast - if you have a radio, try to listen to the forecast in the morning so you can update them (in many ski resorts you will hear it in English as well as the local language!).

Alternatively, you can usually get a printout of the long-range forecast at the Tourist Office, which can then be pinned up in your chalet.

Conduct in the chalet

You will quickly learn that all guests are different and appreciate a different approach. However, some good rules to stick by are:

- Be unobtrusive but attentive
- Be friendly and chatty, but only actually 'socialise' with guests if invited
- With particularly demanding guests, grin and bear it, it's only for a week
- Don't let other staff wander in and out of the chalet, it's intrusive and does not put guests at ease.

the little extras

Guest management

Over the course of the season, you will have a wide range of guests with varying backgrounds and personalities staying in your chalet. Some will be more easily pleased than others!

Part of the secret of happy guests is to ensure their week gets off to a good start. There are some variables that are outside of your control, for example, the weather, a delayed flight, or a bad journey to resort. These can all result in unhappy guests on arrival, and it is then vital to turn your guests' mood around:

- Be there to greet them and help with luggage
- Welcome them with goodies like tea, coffee, vin chaud and cake
- Sympathise with any hiccups they've had during transfer
- Be attentive and do whatever you can to meet their needs on arrival!

It is likely at some point during your season, you will have guests with other complaints, perhaps about food, or their room. In these instances, be polite and as helpful as possible. If you are unable to resolve the situation, you can usually refer them onto your rep or resort manager.

In general however you will find that most guests are not only friendly, but are genuinely interested in you and your motivations for doing a ski season. Be prepared for the same questions week in, week out, and try to respond with the same enthusiasm each time. If your guests like you, then it can help you to get away with any minor hiccups that may occur during their stay.

Guest bar/refreshments

Please note that whether you are able to offer the following services will depend on the policy of your employer. Always check first before offering any of these options.

Many chalets operate an honesty bar, both a good service for guests, and a way of making extra cash. Quite simply, you buy a stock of cans of soft drinks or mixers, bottles of water, and chocolate bars in bulk at the supermarket. You then charge your guests a fixed rate per item, eg 1 Euro, then buy more stock with the profit you make.

Always ensure the guests are aware of this service, and how it operates - usually you can leave a book somewhere in the communal area with all guest names in it, and they make a note when they take something. You can then ask them to settle up their 'bill' before dinner on their last day.

Packed lunches

While some guests are happy to pay inflated prices for lunch on the mountain, others are happy with a baguette sandwich in the sun! You may be able to offer packed lunches, for example sandwich, piece of fruit, and mini chocolate bar. You can buy the fruit, bread, chocolate etc. along with your honesty bar purchases. Don't forget to offer this for departure day also - you'll usually have a few takers!

translations

ENGLISH	FRENCH	GERMAN	ITALIAN
MEAT/FISH	**VIANDE/POISSON**	**FLEISCH/FISCH**	**CARNE/PESCE**
Bacon	Poitrine	Speck	Pancetta
Beef	Boeuf	Rindfleisch	Manzo
Chicken	Poulet	Hähnchen	Pollo
Cod	Morue	Dorsch	Merluzzo
Crab	Crabe	Krebs	Granchio
Duck	Canard	Ente	Anatra
Fish	Poisson	Fisch	Pesce
Ham	Jambon	Schinken	Prosciutto
Lamb	Agneau	Lamm	Agnello
Pâté	Pâté	Pastete	Pasticcio
Pork	Porc	Schwein	Maiale
Prawns	Crevettes	Krabben	Gambero
Salmon	Saumon	Lachs	Salmone
Sausage	Saucisse	Wurst	Salsiccia
Trout	Truite	Forelle	Trota
Tuna	Thon	Thunfisch	Tonno
Turkey	Dinde	Pute	Tacchino
Veal	Veau	Kalbfleisch	Vitello
FRUIT	**FRUITS**	**FRÜCHTE**	**FRUTTI**
Almond	Amande	Mandel	Mandorla
Apple	Pomme	Apfel	Mela
Apricot	Abricot	Aprikose	Albicocca
Banana	Banane	Banane	Banana
Cherry	Cerise	Kirsch	Ciliegia
Chesnut	Marron	Kastanie	Marrone
Coconut	Noix de Coco	Kokonuss	Noce di cocco
Date	Datte	Date	Dattero
Grapefruit	Pamplemousse	Pampelmuse	Pompelmo
Grapes	Raisin	Traube	Uva
Hazelnuts	Noisettes	Haselnuss	Nocciola
Walnut	Noix	Walnuss	Noce
Lemon	Citron	Zitrone	Limone
Melon	Melon	Melone	Melone
Orange	Orange	Apfelsine/Orange	Arancia
Peach	Pêche	Pfirsich	Pesca
Peanut	Cacahuète	Erdnuss	Arachide
Pear	Poire	Birne	Pera
Pineapple	Ananas	Ananas	Ananax
Plum	Prune	Pflaume	Susina
Prune	Pruneau	Backpflaume	Prugna
Raisins	Raisins secs	Korinthen	Zibibbi
Raspberry	Framboise	Himbeere	Lampone
Strawberry	Fraise	Erdbeere	Fragola
Tangerine	Mandarine	Madarine	Mandarino

translations

ENGLISH	FRENCH	GERMAN	ITALIAN
VEGETABLES	**LEGUMES**	**GEMÜSE**	**VERDURE**
Artichoke	Artichaud	Artischocke	Carciofo
Aubergine	Augerbine	Aubergine	Melanzana
Basil	Basilic	Basilienkraut	Basilico
Bayleaf	Laurier	Lorbeerblatt	Alloro
Broccoli	Brocoli	Spargelkohl	Broccolo
Brussels Sprouts	Choux de Bruxelles	Rosenkohl	Cavolini
Cabbage	Chou	Kraut	Cavolo
Carrots	Carottes	Karotten	Carota
Cauliflower	Chou-fleur	Blumenkohl	Cavolfiore
Celery	Céleri	Sellerie	Sedano
Chervil	Cerfeuil	Kerbel	Cerfoglio
Chick peas	Pois chiches	Kichererbse	Ceci
Chicory	Endives	Endiven	Indivie
Chives	Ciboulette	Schnittlauch	Cipollina
Courgette	Courgette	Zucchini	Zucchino
Cucumber	Concombre	Gurke	Cetriolo
Fennel	Fenouille	Fenchel	Finocchio
French beans	Haricots verts	Zwergbohnen	Flagioli verdi
Garlic	Aïl	Knoblauch	Aglio
Ginger	Gingenvre	Ingwer	Zenzero
Leeks	Poireaux	Lauch	Porros
Lettuce	Laitue	Salat	Lattuga
Mint	Menthe	Münze	Menta
Mushrooms	Champignons	Pilzen	Fungi
Onions	Oignons	Zwiebeln	Cipolle
Parsley	Persil	Petersilie	Prezzemolo
Peas	Petits pois	Erbsen	Piselli
Pepper (sweet)	Poivron	Paprika	Peperoni
Potatoes	Pommes de terre	Kartoffeln	Patate
Rosemary	Romarin	Rosmarin	Rosmarino
Sage	Sauge	Salbei	Salvia
Spinach	Epinards	Spinat	Spinaci
Tarragon	Estragon	Estragon	Dragoncello
Tomatoes	Tomates	Tomaten	Pomodori
DAIRY PRODUCTS	**PRODUITS LAITIERS**	**MOLKEREI-PRODUKTE**	**PRODOTTI LATTAII**
Milk	Lait	Milch	Latte
Butter	Beurre	Butter	Burro
Cheese	Fromage	Käse	Formaggio
Cream	Crème	Rahm/Sahne	Crema
Margarine	Margarine	Margarine	Margarina
Yoghurt	Yaourt	Joghurt	Yogurt

conversion charts

Metric/Imperial Measurements

To convert Imperial to Metric, multiply by the amount shown. For Metric to Imperial, divide by the same amount.

Length (inches/mms & cms)	Multiply by
Inches into millimetres	25.40
Inches into centimetres	2.540

Volume (fl oz & pints/mls & litres)	Multiply by
Teaspoons into millilitres	4.930
Tablespoons into millitres	14.78
UK pints into litres	0.568
UK fluid ounces into cubic centimetres	28.41
US pints into litres	0.470

Weight: (lbs & oz/g & kgs)	Multiply by
Ounces into grams	28.34
Ounces into kilograms	0.028
Pounds into kilograms	0.453

Example Conversions

Length		Volume		Weights	
¼	5	2 fl oz	55ml	½ oz	10g
½	1cm	5 (¼ pint)	150	1	25
1	2.5	10 (½ pint)	275	4	110
2	5	1 pint	570	9	250
4	10	1¾	1 litre	10	275
8	20	2½	1.5	3lb	1.35kg

Temperatures

Temperature	Gas Mark	Celsius°C	Fahrenheit°F	Continental Electric Cooker
Very Cool	¼	110°C	225°F	
	½	130°C	250°F	
Cool	1	140°C	275°F	1 (140°C)
	2	150°C	300°F	2 (150°C)
Moderate	3	160°C	325°F	3 (170°C)
	4	180°C	350°F	4 (180°C)
Moderately Hot	5	190°C	375°F	5 (190°C)
	6	200°C	400°F	6 (200°C)
Hot	7	220°C	425°F	7 (220°C)
	8	230°C	450°F	8 (240°C)
				9 (240°C)
				10 (250°C)

recipe index

Canapés, Soups and Starters

Main Courses

recipe index

natives clothing

- FULLY SECURE, ONLINE SHOPPING

- GREAT STYLES, GREAT PRICES

- FAST AND EFFICIENT DELIVERY

- 30 DAY NO QUESTIONS ASKED
  GUARANTEE

- BESPOKE DESIGNS AND GROUP
  DISCOUNTS

- OTHER GREAT BRANDS INCLUDING
  EIRA, FREEFORM & POWDERMONKEY

Natives Merchandise is also available in the UK at the Birmingham and London Ski Shows, and in the Alps at Freeride.fr (Meribel and Courchevel) and Invasion (Chamonix).

10% DISCOUNT VOUCHER

This voucher entitles you to a 10% discount on any Natives Hoody or T bought through the Natives online store.

How to claim your discount:
1. Make your choice of garment from our superb range of hoodys and Ts
2. Add the garment to your online basket and 'Check Out'
3. Select 'Invoice and Payment by Delivery' as your payment method
4. Send in a cheque for the total less 10%, together with this voucher
5. Alternatively, call us on 08700 463377, quoting ref. CB08 and pay by card